REMEMBER THE SABBATH DAY

THE ENDURING APPLICABILITY OF THE FOURTH COMMANDMENT

TRANSLATED WORKS OF PIERRE VIRET

The Catechism of Pierre Viret

The Christian and the Magistrate

His Glorious Bride

Jesus Christ, the Believer's Comfort and Joy

Letters of Comfort to the Persecuted Church

Marvelous Trinity

Simple Exposition of the Christian Faith

Pierre Viret: the Angel of the Reformation

VIRET DECALOGUE COMMENTARY SERIES

No Other God

Nothing Like God

Taking His Name in Vain

Remember the Sabbath Day

Honor thy Father and Mother

Thou Shalt Not Kill: A Plea for Life

Thou Shalt Not Commit Adultery

Thou Shalt Not Steal

Defend the Truth

Thou Shalt Not Covet

REMEMBER THE SABBATH DAY

THE ENDURING APPLICABILITY OF THE FOURTH COMMANDMENT

by Pierre Viret

with a sermon by John Calvin

Translated by R. A. Sheats

Psalm 78 Ministries

www.psalm78ministries.com

Remember the Sabbath Day: the Enduring Applicability of the Fourth Commandment

by Pierre Viret, with a sermon by John Calvin

Translated by R. A. Sheats

Second edition

Published by:

Psalm 78 Ministries
P. O. Box 950
Monticello, FL 32345

psalm78ministries.com

Biblical quotations are taken from the King James Version of the Holy Scriptures. Divine pronouns have been capitalized.

TABLE OF CONTENTS

Translator's Note

The text of this book has been translated from Pierre Viret's commentary on the Fourth Commandment, which was originally published in his work on the Ten Commandments published in French under the title *Exposition familiere sur les Dix Commandemens de la Loy* (Geneva, 1554). It later appeared in an enlarged 1564 edition under the title *Instruction Chrestienne en la doctrine de la loy et de l'Evangile,* printed in Geneva by Jean Rivery. The text of this book has been translated from the 1564 edition.

Viret wrote this work as a conversation between two fictitious individuals, Timothy and Daniel. *Remember the Sabbath Day,* the first English translation of Viret's commentary on the Fourth Commandment, opens just after Daniel has finished explaining the meaning of the first three commandments to Timothy. The conversation now proceeds to the fourth and final commandment remaining in the first table of the Law.

A year after Viret's work on the Ten Commandments came to print, John Calvin began preaching through the book of Deuteronomy to his congregation in Geneva. The text which forms the final chapter of this book is taken from his sermon on Deuteronomy 5:12-14, translated from the published version *Sermons de M. Jean Calvin sur le v. livre de Moyse nommé Deuteronome* (Thomas Courteau, Geneva, 1567).

All direct Scripture quotations have been set forth in the King James Version. When Viret cites Scripture but does not quote verbatim, his wording has been retained and the Scriptural reference placed in parentheses. Explanatory footnotes and Scripture references in brackets have also been added for clarification and do not appear in the original French text. Chapter headings have been added and the text has been abridged.

ONE

The Fourth Commandment of the Law

"Remember the sabbath day, to keep it holy. Six days shalt thou labour, and do all thy work: but the seventh day is the sabbath of the Lord *thy God: in it thou shalt not do any work, thou, nor thy son, nor thy daughter, thy manservant, nor thy maidservant, nor thy cattle, nor thy stranger that is within thy gates: for in six days the* Lord *made heaven and earth, the sea, and all that in them is, and rested the seventh day: wherefore the* Lord *blessed the sabbath day, and hallowed it." — Exodus 20:8-11*

TIMOTHY: We've already proceeded quite far in the exposition of the commandments of the first table, for we've already finished with three of them. The fourth is all that remains, for it's the last of them all. It reminds me of the sequence, agreement, and connection you showed it to have with the others preceding it when you spoke of the order which God employed in the disposition of the commandments of this first table and the unity of the matters contained in it. I'm certain that these things will be revealed with even greater clarity after you explain the meaning of this commandment and after you've more fully explained the reasons and the purpose why God gave it. Therefore tell me first how many parts the commandment contains, what each one means, and in what order they're laid out. For it seems to me that this commandment contains many things.

DANIEL: God first sets forth the commandment in general and declares what He requires by it when He says "Remember the sabbath day, to keep it holy."

Second, He shows more particularly which day He means by the *sabbath day*, and in what way He desires it to be different from the other days, in order that there might be no confusion and that the people might not be left at liberty to choose this according to their own pleasure. He also shows in general how every man must conduct himself both on this day as well as on all the others when He adds: "Six days shalt thou labour, and do all thy work: but the seventh day is the sabbath of the LORD thy God."

Third, He explains in detail what He briefly mentioned previously regarding the duty of every man, and declares in part what it means to sanctify this day of rest. He reveals spiritual rest—which He requires above all—by the figure of external rest when He says: "in it thou shalt not do any work, thou, nor thy son, nor thy daughter, thy manservant, nor thy maidservant, nor thy cattle, nor thy stranger that is within thy gates,"—that is, the stranger who dwells among you, according to the Hebrew manner of speaking.

Afterward He sets forth the reason why He chose this seventh day rather than any other day, saying: "for in six days the LORD made heaven and earth, the sea, and all that in them is, and rested the seventh day: wherefore the LORD blessed the sabbath day, and hallowed it."

Now we must examine all the words by which this commandment is set forth to us.

TIMOTHY: I would certainly like to do so.

HOW THE OBSERVANCE OF THIS COMMANDMENT IS REQUIRED AND COMMENDED IN THE HOLY SCRIPTURES

DANIEL: First, you must note that He says "Remember" or "You must remember to sanctify the sabbath day," and doesn't simply say, "Sanctify the sabbath day." This is a type of commanding which is neither light nor ordinary, nor one which concerns unimportant things. By this He reveals that what He desires to set forth is of great importance and is of such a nature that He wills that it be so imprinted on our hearts that it will never be forgotten but instead will be observed exactly as He commands. Therefore we ought to think on it day and night. For there is nothing worse than forgetting God's commandments, nor anything more dangerous or which further removes us from Him and the keeping of them. Because of this we can rightly say that the forgetting of God's commandments is also the forgetting of God and the beginning and source of all transgression. Therefore *remembrance* is commanded us with good reason, by which the Lord clearly declares to us in this commandment that He requires a proper disposition of the heart and a heart well-disposed toward Him and the observance of His commandments much more than the simple outward rest and cessation of physical labor which concern the ceremonial observance of the Sabbath.

This is why there is no commandment in all the Law which He mentions more solemnly or which is commended more diligently in the books of the prophets. Nor is there any commandment about which the Lord raises greater legal complaints and reproaches against those who violate it. For, when He brings charges against the ingratitude of His people and their despising of His Law, the main thing He most often complains of is that they violated and desecrated the sabbaths and days of rest. And, when He desires to call His people back to His obedience, the main thing He commands of them is the observance of this day, as though all His Law were founded on and included in this commandment and as if it all depended entirely on it.

This is why Moses said: "Verily My sabbaths ye shall keep: for it is a sign between Me and you throughout your generations; that ye may know that I am the LORD that doth sanctify you. Ye shall keep the sabbath therefore; for it is holy unto you. . . . Wherefore the children of Israel shall keep the sabbath, to observe the sabbath throughout their generations, for a perpetual covenant. It is a sign between Me and the children of Israel for ever" (Ex. 31:13-14, 16-17; Lev. 19:30; 26:2).

Ezekiel also said as much: "I gave them My sabbaths, to be a sign between Me and them, that they might know that I am the Lord that sanctify them" (Eze. 20:12). And immediately afterward He says: "My sabbaths they greatly polluted" (Eze. 20:13). He reproaches them with this matter many times in this same chapter with grave curses. Then, when He wishes to summarize it all for them, He says expressly: "Hallow My sabbaths; and they shall be a sign between Me and you, that ye may know that I am the Lord your God" (Eze. 20:20). Again and again He reproaches them for their contempt and violation of this commandment.

Likewise the Levites spoke in the book of Nehemiah as if the entirety of the Law were included in this observance of the Day of Rest, saying before all the church of Israel: "[Thou] madest known unto them Thy holy sabbath, and commandedst them precepts, statutes, and laws, by the hand of Moses Thy servant" (Neh. 9:14).

Also, God truly showed in what reverence and obedience He desires this day to be observed by the great severity He displayed against the wretched transgressor who was condemned to be put to death simply because he gathered wood on the Day of Rest, as is mentioned in the fourth book of Moses (Num. 15:32-36). By this He has also revealed what punishment awaits those who violate the true spiritual Day of Rest and who employ themselves in much worse works and much more offensive labors.

SOME DIFFICULTIES TO CONSIDER REGARDING WHY THE OBSERVANCE OF THE SABBATH DAY IS SO EXPRESSLY COMMENDED, AND ABOVE ALL WHY IT IS PLACED IN THE DECALOGUE

TIMOTHY: Why is there such great severity and such high praises and commendations by which the observance of this day is so expressly commended? Does this commandment contain something even greater and more excellent than the others which we spoke of before? In my opinion it doesn't appear to be greater or more excellent. Nor does it seem to more closely deal with the honor of God than the others. But, to the contrary, it seems that this commandment concerns nothing more than a ceremony which ought now to be abolished among Christians, seeing that we are no longer under the shadows of the ceremonial law to which the Jews were subject. For, since Jesus Christ—who is the Truth and Substance of these shadows—has delivered us from them by the revelation of the Gospel, we have a liberty in these things that the Jews didn't possess.

Therefore I'm surprised at this commandment, particularly because of these three things:

First, why did God place it among the commandments of the Decalogue which rightly pertain to the mind, morals, and character of believers?

Second, why did He put it in such a place of importance among the commandments of the first table, which are the main commandments of all the Law? Why didn't He content Himself with simply putting it among the ceremonial laws, seeing that it appears to pertain better to them than to the moral Law?

Third, why is this commandment more greatly esteemed than any other commandment in the books of the prophets, seeing that its ceremonial aspect would one day be abolished as it is today? For, though we celebrate Sunday instead of the Jewish Sabbath, yet we don't observe it under such subjection and necessity and with such ceremonies and superstitions as the Jews did, knowing the liberty we have in it through Jesus Christ.

THE SPIRITUAL MEANING OF THIS COMMANDMENT, AND THE REST AND SANCTIFICATION WHICH GOD REQUIRES BY IT; AND THE OBLIGATION BY WHICH CHRISTIANS ARE STILL BOUND TO KEEP IT AND IN WHAT WAY

DANIEL: These very things which surprise you ought instead to show you that there is a much greater mystery and secret in this command than what appears at first glance; and that, though its ceremony is indeed abolished, yet it still contains many matters to which we are no less bound today than the Jews were bound in their day, which we must diligently consider and discover. We must do this in such a way that we don't return to Judaism by placing ourselves under the bondage of the ceremonial law from which we are delivered by Jesus Christ. Likewise on the other hand we must beware of entirely casting off the matters which God wills for us to remain bound to.

TIMOTHY: I would truly like to understand this.

DANIEL: To understand it better, we must bear in mind what we've already said of the connection and unity of the preceding commandments with this one and the matters contained in them. For what the Lord requires (not only in these preceding commandments but also in all the others that follow and in His entire Law in general) can't be accomplished in us and by us unless we observe all the things required of us in this commandment.

For how can we truly satisfy all these things if we don't first renounce ourselves and our own will and all our own wisdom, desires, and corrupt nature in such a way that we don't do anything by our own works but that we allow God to work in us, following His Spirit and not our own? This is the first thing that is required of us in this commandment and is the rest which is commanded us (which has been symbolized by physical and outward rest, which is the ceremony contained in this commandment). For this reason when the Lord speaks of this commandment He often uses the word *sanctify* or *hallow*, sometimes commanding us to sanctify it and sometimes saying that He is the Lord our God who sanctifies us (Ex. 20:11; 31:13; Eze. 20:12, 20). By this He clearly declares that, just as He is Holy, so He also requires us to be holy, as He has commanded in other places. We can't do this unless we and all of our heart are totally consecrated to Him by the means we just mentioned and unless we entirely submit ourselves to His holy will and leave ourselves to be completely governed by Him.

On this you must note that there are three types of rest to consider which are contained and represented in this commandment:

The first is the external and physical rest which pertains to the ceremonial aspect of this commandment.

The second is the internal and spiritual rest represented by the physical rest which we just mentioned.

The third is the heavenly and eternal rest which is the completion and consummation of the two preceding rests, which we'll celebrate fully and perfectly after this life in heavenly glory, as we'll more fully explain later. Meanwhile this spiritual rest which is represented for us by the ceremonial rest contained in this commandment (and which is like the beginning of the eternal rest that we await after this life) must serve us as a sacrament of regeneration and sanctification by which we are reminded of our original nature which is utterly corrupt and of our need to be regenerated and renewed by the Spirit of God. We are also reminded that we can't do any good except as God works His works in us, following what Jesus Christ said: "That which is born of the flesh is flesh; and that which is born of the Spirit is spirit" (John 3:6). For this reason He said that we must be born again if we desire to enter into the Kingdom of Heaven.

Secondly, we are also reminded of an honor that God shows His people more than all others, in that He sanctifies them to Himself in order to write His Law upon their hearts and inward parts and make them walk in His commandments, just as He promised by Jeremiah and Ezekiel (Jer. 32:38-40; Eze. 11:19-20; 36:26-27, Heb. 8:10).

THOSE WHO ONLY OBSERVE THE CEREMONY OF THIS COMMANDMENT DO NOT TRULY OBSERVE THE COMMANDMENT OR THE REST COMMANDED IN IT ACCORDING TO THE HOLY SPIRIT'S MEANING; AND HOW THE TRUE OBSERVANCE OF IT LIES IN A SPIRITUAL REST SYMBOLIZED BY THE OUTWARD CEREMONY

TIMOTHY: Therefore it follows therefore that whoever only observes the outward ceremonial rest, without worrying themselves about what is represented by it, in no way fulfills this commandment or the purpose for which it was commanded.

On the other hand, whoever has within himself what is represented by the ceremony, and who fulfills it in truth, truly observes the commandment even if he omits the ceremonial aspect, which is no more than the shadow of the reality which he possesses.[1]

DANIEL: It's true. Isaiah indeed also declares that this is the true observance of the Day of Rest that God requires of us when he said: "If thou turn away thy foot from the sabbath, from doing thy pleasure on My holy day; and call the sabbath a delight, the holy of the LORD, honourable; and shalt honour Him, not doing thine own ways, nor finding thine own pleasure, nor speaking thine own words: then shalt thou delight thyself in the LORD" (Isa. 58:13-14). You can clearly understand by these words that God requires a genuine mortification of ourselves for the observance of His rest, by which we so renounce our own will and our own works that nothing of ourselves remains in it but that all that remains is of Him—and not only for one day, but for all days forever.

Thus (as is clearly revealed in the epistle to the Hebrews) this Day of Rest is the figure and the beginning firstly of the true

---

[1] Viret isn't here annulling the physical rest included in this commandment, but is instead emphasizing the importance of the true and proper fulfilling of its spiritual reality. On this point Calvin notes: "We mustn't think that [physical rest] was the point God was aiming at, for His main purpose wasn't to have one day in seven in which everyone stopped working in order that they might catch their breath and not always be laboring in such a way that they were exhausted; this wasn't the reason why God chose to ordain this Sabbath Day. But He did this in order that believers might understand that they ought to live in such a holy way that they rest from all their own lusts and desires so that God might work entirely in them. As for the [external or physical] rest, this is a nice fringe benefit, as it's commonly called." John Calvin, *Sermons de M. Jean Calvin sur le v. livre de Moyse nommé Deuteronome* (Geneva, 1567), page 198.

spiritual rest that we've already begun in this world, and secondly of the grand Rest of God in us and of us in God, which we call heavenly and eternal, which will be continued from rest to rest and will be an everlasting ordinance, as Isaiah testifies (Isa. 66:23; Heb. 4:3-10).

In the meantime we must so labor to mortify our flesh by following the admonitions which are so often given us—particularly by Paul—in order that we might each be able to say with him: "But God forbid that I should glory, save in the cross of our Lord Jesus Christ, by whom the world is crucified unto me, and I unto the world" (Gal. 6:14). For we will only ever sanctify the Lord's Day of Rest spiritually as it must be sanctified when we are utterly dead and crucified to sin and sin to us, so much so that it has no more strength in us than a dead or crucified man would.

And, because we can never find in ourselves a mortification so perfect while we live in this world without always feeling within our flesh the thorns of sin, we must continually groan and cry out to God, feeling and recognizing in ourselves what Paul testified of himself, saying: "For we know that the law is spiritual: but I am carnal, sold under sin. For that which I do I allow not: for what I would, that do I not; but what I hate, that do I." And further he says: "For I know that in me (that is, in my flesh,) dwelleth no good thing: for to will is present with me; but how to perform that which is good I find not. For the good that I would I do not: but the evil which I would not, that I do." And then: "I find then a law, that, when I would do good, evil is present with me. For I delight in the law of God after the inward man: but I see another law in my members, warring against the law of my mind, and bringing me into captivity to the law of sin which is in my members. O wretched man that I am! who shall deliver me from the body of this death?" (Rom. 7:14-24.) An understanding of this will serve us to always better prepare ourselves for a more perfect sanctifying of the Day of Rest.

TWO

The Day of Rest, the Guardian of the Faith

HOW THE MINISTRY OF THE CHURCH IS COMMENDED BY GOD IN THIS COMMANDMENT; AND HOW THIS COMMANDMENT IS GIVEN TO GUARD AND PRESERVE ALL THE COMMANDMENTS WHICH PRECEDE IT AND ALL THE LAW

TIMOTHY: This Sabbath will be lovely and grand.

DANIEL: It's true. Consequently, to accomplish this spiritual and eternal rest, there are many things required.

TIMOTHY: What are these things?

DANIEL: Man, because he is blinded by sin, is so corrupt in his mind, understanding, and will that he can't even understand the things of God or have any good desire for them unless his nature is regenerated and he is instructed and taught by the Spirit of God. Therefore it's necessary for him to have some means of obtaining this regeneration and instruction. God has given him the means by the ministry of His Word and His sacraments which He ordained for all time in His church, under which we must include all the laws and ordinances which He has established for His divine worship and all the order and discipline by which He wills to govern His Church, which can't be preserved except by means of this ministry. This is why the Law and its doctrine "of old time hath in every city them that preach" it in the church of Israel, "being read in the synagogues every sabbath day," as James testified in the Jerusalem Council (Acts 15:21). For, if this ministry were abolished, the ruin of all these things would follow. Indeed, we had far too much experience of this during the times of the darkness and ignorance we lived in under the papacy. For what was the reason why all Christian religion was utterly transformed into more of a superstition than either Judaism or paganism? Wasn't it because of the fact that the papacy abandoned this ministry by which Christian instruction must be maintained in the Church and the Church governed by it?

TIMOTHY: It is true. For everything was transformed into chants in which neither the wise nor the ignorant had any understanding at all of what was being chanted; or at least they understood very little, and the profit that each received was truly meager. For, in all the divine worship which is conducted in the papacy (besides the entertainments that exist simply for the pleasing of the flesh, as those who attend the plays and programs), the mind and spirit receive precious little fruit.

DANIEL: You speak the truth. And, because this ministry and the order which God established in His Church can't be preserved as He has required if there is no lawful and legitimate assembly of all the people of God and some proper and convenient time, place, and order for gathering together, God has indeed chosen to ordain a particular day to do this, having regard to the infirmity of men, which we will speak of more fully later.

Therefore we must understand that when He gave this commandment He established within it the safeguards of those commandments which precede it. For, seeing that He wills to make Himself known, so He also wills to have a Church to whom He imparts His goodness forever and in which He is known and glorified. For this reason, after He gave in the first commandment the law concerning the knowledge which we must have of Him and the will and disposition of our heart toward Him; and in the second and third the declaration and confession which must be made of this both by outward act and by mouth; so He wills that this knowledge and confession be proclaimed and multiplied by a particular means and ministry by particular persons, and in particular assemblies which He wills to preserve, guard, and defend, no matter how great an effort Satan and tyrants (who are his ministers) might put forth to break up and destroy it. And all this is ordained in order that all might be done in an orderly manner in these assemblies over which God presides by His Word and His Holy Spirit.

HOW PHYSICAL REST IS REQUIRED WITH SPIRITUAL REST IN THIS COMMANDMENT; AND HOW IT IS GIVEN TO SERVE FAITH AND LOVE; AND HOW THE TRANSGRESSION OF THIS COMMANDMENT ENCOMPASSES THE TRANSGRESSION OF THE WHOLE LAW OF GOD

TIMOTHY: From what I understand, you wish to say that, besides this spiritual rest (of which the physical is a picture), God still requires of us a physical rest in order that with the time we employ in our manual labors on other days we might now employ ourselves in the ministry of His Word and divine worship.

DANIEL: This is the second main point which must be noted in this commandment. Besides this we must also understand that God still requires of us a rest bestowed by us on those who are under our charge, to serve by it to the love due to our neighbor, in order that he might also celebrate with us the other rest which serves for faith and divine worship.

Thus you see here how the observance of all the Law and all divine worship is encompassed in this commandment, by which you can understand that the transgression and violation of it is also the transgression of the whole Law and the ruin of all true religion. Thus you mustn't be surprised that God has so greatly commended the observance of this day and if He so grievously punished the transgressors of it. For He doesn't look only to the ceremony but to the disobedience and rebellion committed against His majesty, the contempt of His Word and His divine worship, and the consequences which would follow from it. But, seeing that we'll deal with this more fully in another place, let's return to the original point of spiritual rest.

TIMOTHY: This is a good idea, and afterward we'll return to the other points in order.

THREE

Sanctifying the Day of Rest

HOW WE ALREADY BEGIN THE SPIRITUAL AND ETERNAL REST IN THIS WORLD AND HOW BAPTISM IS A FIGURE OF IT; AND HOW THE WORK OF GOD IN US IS A TRUE REST AND PLEASURE AND NOT A BURDENSOME TASK

DANIEL: We already begin this rest by the mortification of our flesh which is worked daily in us by the Spirit of God by whom we are regenerated, which is also represented to us in baptism, by which we die and are buried and raised with Jesus Christ (Rom. 6:1-4; 4:1-5). For, just as He died for our sins, was buried, and rested in His grave the seventh day (which was the Sabbath), and was then raised for our justification, so also we must die and be buried to sin in order that we might be raised with Jesus Christ to a new life by which we are made new creatures in Him (Matt. 27:57-66; Mark 15:42-47; Luke 23:50-55; John 19:38-42; Rom. 4:24-25; 6:1-4; Col. 2:12; 3:1-4). When we thus fulfill what is represented by our baptism, we then accomplish this commandment by which we aren't commanded simply to rest but only to rest from one work in order to accomplish another.

But, seeing that this work which is required of us in this Day of Rest is so contrary to our nature that we can't accomplish it at all except by the working and power of the Spirit of God, the work is rightly attributed to God and not to us. It is also rightly called *rest* in comparison with the works we do naturally. For in all our labor there is neither travail, hard labor, or trouble in anything at all except in the work of sin and as much as our work is stained by it. For it is sin alone which hinders the rest which we ought to enjoy in God, and it's sin which completely removes rest from us because it incites our will to rebel against God and moves us to treason, enflaming our passions and desires to a bloody war as much as they proceed from Satan who "was a murderer from the beginning" (John 8:44).

But in the work of God there is nothing but true rest, peace, joy, and great delight. For, just as He labors without pain and travail (seeing that there is nothing within Him which partakes of sin or battles against the true righteousness which is natural to Him and of which He is the source and fountain), so also as much as a man more closely approaches this righteousness of God and labors in much greater power by it by means of the Spirit of God, so much less will he have pain and travail, and his labor is for him a grand rest and a great pleasure and delight.

HOW GOD NOT ONLY COMMANDS THE REST OF THE SEVENTH DAY BUT ALSO ITS SANCTIFICATION; AND WHAT THIS SANCTIFICATION MUST BE AND HOW WE MUST CONSIDER IT IN GOD AND IN OURSELVES

TIMOTHY: I think this labor is such as Adam would have had in paradise had he not sinned.

DANIEL: The comparison isn't a poor one. On this you must understand that the Lord, when He desired to show us that the rest which He requires of us mustn't be idleness, didn't simply say "Rest on this day" but said: "Remember the sabbath day, to keep it holy," as if He had said: "Dedicate this day to the holy things which pertain to My glory, and rest from your own works in such a way that you might do Mine, which are holy." On this we must note two points.

TIMOTHY: What is the first?

DANIEL: That we must consider this sanctification in two ways: first in God, and then in us. For, since God has already sanctified this day, what further need is there for man to sanctify it? And how can it be sanctified by him who possesses no sanctification in himself at all, for this proceeds from God alone, who is the Holy of Holies and who alone sanctifies all that is holy and sanctified?

TIMOTHY: Please explain this to me.

DANIEL: Moses has here given us a very clear testimony that this day was sanctified by God not only like all the others, but also by a special sanctification. Now God sanctified this day when He chose it, separated it, and distinguished it from the others in order to particularly dedicate and consecrate it to Himself, to holy works, and to His divine worship, just as He dedicated and consecrated the water in baptism as a sign of His grace and the bread and wine in the Lord's Supper as signs and testimonies of the body and blood of Jesus Christ given over to death for us. This consecration is the prerogative of none but Him alone.

TIMOTHY: What then does He further require of us?

DANIEL: He requires that, following His command, we take as holy what He has sanctified and consecrated in this way and that we dedicate it to His holiness and to good and holy uses, just as He requires of us by His commandment. For this reason you must also note (as the other point which still remains) that He didn't only say "Keep the sabbath holy," but said expressly "Keep the sabbath day holy," to more impress upon us and to make us better understand that He wills that the day itself be holy to us. He doesn't place this difference between days for Himself (as though He had need of days), but rather He does it to make us understand that the holy day also requires a holy work, in order that there might be a suitability between the day and the work to better partake in this new spiritual and eternal rest which is represented by it. For, though it's already begun in us by our regeneration and continues daily by the mortification of our flesh and our earthly members, yet it can't be fully accomplished in us until that time when the kingdom of God will be fully accomplished and perfected in us and when we will know even as we are also known and will see Him face to face, and He will be all in all (Col. 3:1-5; 1 Cor. 13:12; 15:28).

FOUR

The Dangers of Misunderstanding Rest

THE REASONS WHY GOD ONLY ORDAINED ONE DAY TO SYMBOLIZE SPIRITUAL AND ETERNAL REST; AND THE DANGER WHICH EXISTS IN ENCOURAGING MEN TO IDLENESS BY MEANS OF HOLIDAYS AND FEASTS

TIMOTHY: Seeing that this sabbath and spiritual rest represented by this external rest is eternal, why did the Lord only ordain one day to symbolize it? For one day can't begin to compare with an eternity and infinity. Yet it's necessary for the shadows and figures to pertain and correspond to the truth and reality as closely as possible.

Secondly, seeing that this day was also ordained for the preservation of the ministry of the Church and to attend to what is necessary in it, it seems to me that this ministry truly ought to require more of our time and rest than our other occupations. For, even if we occupied ourselves with this every day for the rest of our lives, we still would scarcely have advanced, and would have done our duty but poorly.

DANIEL: There have already been more than five thousand of these days to represent what it signifies. For there is no need for the shadows and figures to be in all ways similar to the truth which they represent; otherwise there would be no difference between them, and the shadows and figures would no longer be shadows and figures, but would be the reality themselves.

Secondly, seeing that this human life is subject to so many necessities for which men must labor daily, the external rest couldn't last long without doing great harm to human life. Therefore God desired to bear with His people in this and content Himself with one day of the week. For, even if every day of human life were employed in such an external rest, the days of this temporal rest still wouldn't perfectly correspond to those of the spiritual and eternal rest because of the difference between temporal and eternal things.

Third, even if it were possible for man to live without work, yet human weakness and the vanity of the human understanding is so great that it is unable to apply itself for very long to the study and meditation of the works of God and divine and heavenly things without wandering hither and yon and becoming lost in daydreams aroused by its imagination, and thus abandoning this meditation in order to devote itself to carnal pleasures in its idleness. For, though the Lord didn't ordain many days for a physical rest, yet we see very few men so perfect that they can dedicate even a single entire day in all the year to the worship of God required in this commandment in such a way that they don't wander to many other things much worse than if they labored with their hands in some useful employment for their own good or for the good of their neighbor.

THE ABUSE WHICH EXISTS IN CHRISTIAN PAPIST HOLIDAYS, AND HOW THEY ARE DEDICATED TO THE DEVIL AND NOT TO GOD

TIMOTHY: We clearly experience what you say on every holiday and feast day. For there are no days of the entire year in which God is more insulted. For there are few people who consider the purpose for which the sabbaths and holidays were appointed and this spiritual rest you mentioned, but instead they assume that the feasts and holidays were ordained simply so that they can pass the time in idleness or employ it in all sorts of dissolute activities, for on these days they are more licentious than on any others.

DANIEL: It's indeed true that Christian papists today celebrate their holidays in the same way that the ancient pagans did. By this they clearly reveal that they've poorly understood what the Lord said: "The seventh day is the sabbath of the LORD thy God." He didn't say, "The seventh day is *your* sabbath" or the sabbath of Abraham, Isaac, or some other patriarch or holy person, but He said that it was *His,* both because He sanctified and consecrated this day and because He ordained it to be a memorial and a sacrament of the rest that He entered into after He finished His work of the creation of the world. By speaking in this way He teaches us two things:

First, this day must be dedicated and consecrated to Him and to His Name' and to no other. For, if He had desired to consecrate and dedicate it—or the other days and feasts which He later ordained—to another, He could very well have ordained them in honor and memory of Abraham, Isaac, Jacob, or others like them, and of their birth, exodus, journeys, and other things worthy of remembrance which were done by them and through them. But, being well aware of man's natural inclination to idolatry, He didn't choose to introduce this custom into His Church, for He knows quite well how natural and easy it is for men to make idols of themselves and of men like themselves, as we see has happened with the pagans who dedicated their feasts to mortal men whom they elevated to the place of God in nearly the same way that the Christian papists have done and still continue to do with their saints.

TIMOTHY: If God had no desire to introduce this custom into the Church of Israel, it seems to me that we have no greater reason to receive it in the Christian Church.

DANIEL: The fruit which follows it bears sufficient testimony to this.

THE PROFIT GAINED FROM PAPAL HOLIDAYS AND FEASTS, AND WHOM THEY BENEFIT; AND THE DISTINCTION PAPISTS DRAW BETWEEN THE ACTIVE AND CONTEMPLATIVE LIFE; AND HOW BOTH ARE REQUIRED OF ALL TRUE CHRISTIANS

DANIEL: When all is well considered, where the church isn't reformed by the Word of God, there are none who receive any profit from the feasts except the priests. For these are the days of their grand marches and festivals, particularly the holidays which they dedicate to dead men (in imitation of the pagans) under the name and title of *saints,* from which they accrue all the gain of their merchandise and from which all who trade with them gain loss and harm to themselves.

But let's leave the normal people aside and consider the more spiritual and contemplative people. What greater dreamers has the world ever had than monks and nuns who boast themselves of the contemplative and monastic life and the state of perfection? And what people have ever been given to more abominations and all manner of villainy and wicked living than those who wish to be considered spiritual, pious, and religious and who have chosen a life of idleness under the guise of attending to the worship of God; as if there were no other worship of God except in their life which they call "contemplative" and "a life of meditation," as if the life which they call "active" or "secular" were utterly condemned by God and as if God wasn't honored or served in such a life at all?

God didn't divide men's lives up in this way, assigning to some a life of contemplation and to others an active or secular life. But He willed for every man to lead both a meditative and an active life in order that every one might put his meditations into practice to the glory of God. For this reason He commanded all men both to labor and to rest (for He wills to be served and honored by both means), and bound every man individually to the observance of all the commandments contained in the two tables of the Law. For He didn't give one table to some men and the other table to others, but instead He desires every man to be employed in His service and in the service of one's neighbor out of love for Him in every way that He has commanded. (We will deal with this more fully in the exposition of the second table.)

And, because He was well aware of the danger which idleness brings on man, He was content to command him to cease from his other works only one day of the week in order to wholly dedicate that day to spiritual matters, leaving the other days of the week to his liberty to do the works necessary for this life. This is why He said: "Six days shalt thou labour, and do all thy work: but the seventh day is the sabbath [or rest] of the LORD thy God."

THE LABOR COMMANDED ON THE SIX DAYS OF THE WEEK, AND THE REST PERMITTED IN THEM, AND THE HOLIDAYS AND FEASTS WHICH CAN BE CELEBRATED

TIMOTHY: Has God so commanded labor on these six days that it would never be permissible to have a holiday on any other day besides the seventh? And is He content if man simply attends to the meditation of divine things only on this seventh day?

DANIEL: Seeing that this seventh day was a figure of the rest that we ought always to have in God, we mustn't doubt that He requires us to attend to it continually. For this reason He ordained this seventh day as a sign to instruct us once a week in what we ought to be doing perpetually. And, because human weakness is so great in us that we are always more given to temporal things than to spiritual, He permitted us to labor in all things for the majority of our time in order to better assist us in our infirmity and to better remove all excuse from us; on condition that we aren't so given to physical things that we won't willingly leave them (at least during some specific times) to completely employ ourselves in His spiritual service and for the edification of our souls and of His Church, without any other distractions arising from our earthly affairs.

Also, when He said "Six days shalt thou labour," He

didn't forbid us from resting within these six days if necessity requires it. Nor likewise did He forbid us from taking a holiday if it's sometimes expedient for the edification of the Church, to attend to fastings, prayers, and the Word of God according to circumstances and according to the needs of various times, places, and persons, as long as all is done without superstition and is done decently and in good ecclesiastical order, just as the former servants of God did and according to the form and examples we have in the Holy Scriptures.

HOW GOD NOT ONLY COMMANDED HIS PEOPLE TO REST AT THE TIME ORDAINED BY HIM, BUT ALSO TO WORK IN THE TIME HE HAS PERMITTED FOR LABOR

TIMOTHY: In the manner that you take these words, it seems to me that they carry a permission to work rather than an express command.

DANIEL: We can truly understand it as you say. But we must also consider that, since God condemns idleness in man and commands him to labor (though He doesn't require it without exception in giving the law of rest), so also He didn't desire to give the law of rest without likewise giving a law for labor, in order that He might also put into execution the commandment in which it is said: "In the sweat of thy face shalt thou eat bread," and again: "Cursed is the ground for thy sake; in sorrow shalt thou eat of it all the days of thy life" (Gen. 3:19, 17). Thus, seeing that man was given this commandment, it isn't lawful for him to live in idleness and only do what pleases him. Instead he is required to work when he has the opportunity and the means, without ever remaining idle, so that when he rests, he rests out of necessity and in the manner which is prescribed for him by the Lord.

Indeed, this command is truly quite sensible. For what would become of man in this natural corruption which is in him if he were permitted to live in idleness and at his own pleasure?

Therefore every man is commanded to work in the days and means in which labor is permitted him. And not only this, but it is also enjoined upon every man to labor at their work according to each person's particular position and calling in order that there might not be confusion, but instead that all might govern themselves according to their positions and offices.

This is why, just as the Lord gives us His own example and His own authority for rest, He also does the same for labor in order that we might follow Him in both of these things, doing our works according to our calling as He has done His and resting from our labors just as He rested from His. Thus what He says here is the same as if He had said: "I have set you six days for work, but not as though I've expressly commanded you to work every single moment of these six days in whatever labor you wish without any respite at all no matter what necessity might arise. But it will be lawful for you to labor in these days in all your works on condition that this seventh day be entirely dedicated to Me and that you complete whatever labor you must do on the other days."

For, just as this rest isn't expressly commanded on the Sabbath Day in such a way that it's never lawful to do any work on it when necessity requires it (as Jesus Christ gave us an example of), so also labor isn't expressly commanded throughout the other days in such a way that it's never lawful to rest in them as every person's need might require.

TIMOTHY: Now I understand this well.

FIVE

A Look at the Old Testament Feasts

THE OTHER FEASTS COMMANDED BY GOD TO THE PEOPLE OF ISRAEL BESIDES THE ORDINARY WEEKLY SABBATH

DANIEL: Since God Himself commanded feasts and holidays other than the rest of this seventh day, it indeed appears that He didn't command labor in these six days in such a way that it was never lawful to rest in them—though He didn't command many feasts, and some of them even fell on this seventh day. For, besides these weekly days of rest, there were only seven other days in the entire rest of the year in which all work was forbidden. The feast of Passover lasted an entire week, but it was only on the first and the last day that it was commanded to rest entirely from all ordinary labor. The same thing was done during the feast of Tabernacles (which began on the fifteenth day of the seventh month), of which it was expressly commanded in the law that at a certain time the book of the Law must be read before all the people, as it was done in the times of Nehemiah after the return from the Babylonian captivity (Deut. 31:9-13; Neh. 8:1-3). The feast of First Fruits (called Pentecost by the Greeks because it was celebrated fifty days after Passover) and likewise the feast of Trumpets which fell on the first day of the seventh month, and that of the Day of Atonement which fell on the tenth of that month, only had one day each for the three of them.

TIMOTHY: There weren't many feasts, then. Therefore the Jews couldn't complain that they were too heavily burdened or that their labors were left undone because of them.

THE TIMES ORDAINED BY GOD FOR THE FEASTS, AND THE SUPPORT OF THE PEOPLE IN THEM, AND THE REASON FOR THEIR INSTITUTION

DANIEL: Besides this we must also consider that the majority of these feasts fell during the time that the fruits of the earth were already harvested and the main labors of the entire year were finished. For their seventh month corresponded to our September, in which both harvest and grape-picking (which are the main seasons for gathering in the fruits of the year) were accomplished, particularly in those countries which have temperate and warm climates.

TIMOTHY: As far as I can see, by this God declared to His people that He cared for them and looked after their needs, for He gave them neither any large occasion for idleness nor any great impediment to the works necessary for this life.

DANIEL: There is still another point which confirms what you say, for even the other feasts besides those of the seventh month were ordained in times in which the people were less pressed by their labor. For Passover always fell in a month which corresponded to our month of March or April, in which the people weren't engaged in either planting or harvesting. And then Pentecost followed the harvest. By doing this God greatly eased the burden of His people and also admonished them before and after the fruits of the earth were gathered in to recognize their Lord by whose mercy they had gathered in the possessions of the earth, and to render homage and thanksgiving to Him for His blessings.

TIMOTHY: It seems to me that those who have so greatly

multiplied the holidays among Christians didn't consider the model and example that God set in this matter. For it would have been much better if they had considered the wellbeing of the Christian people in these things, as God did the people of Israel, for the reasons that we've set forth.

DANIEL: You speak well.

THE FEAST OF THE DEDICATION OF THE JEWS CALLED ENCAENIA, AND ITS ORDINANCE

TIMOTHY: If I'm not mistaken, I think you left out a feast which is called *Encaenia* (or *Dedication*) in the New Testament; you didn't mention it. Yet John testifies that our Lord Jesus Christ celebrated it with the other Jews, for he clearly shows that He went up to Jerusalem at that time just as the other Jews did (John 10:22-23).

DANIEL: Though I might have anticipated your question, yet I didn't add this feast to the others because it wasn't commanded in the law as they were. Nor was it ordained in the time of Moses or the other patriarchs and prophets, but a long time afterward, even during the time of the Babylonian captivity—that is, during the time of the Maccabees. It was ordained after the worship of God was restored and the church was reformed when the Maccabees were victorious over their enemies and when they gathered the outcasts of the church of Israel which had nearly all been driven away by the wars and destruction of their enemies, and particularly of Antiochus. And, because God showed this grace and mercy to this poor people and because they received so great a joy in this journey, this day has remained in perpetual memory and solemnity in Israel, so much so that the Jews, following the example of their ancestors, by Jewish superstition, still celebrate it today on the twenty-fifth day of the month which corresponds in part to our December. And, because the church of Israel was from then on considered renewed or rebuilt and consecrated anew, this feast was to the Jews like a feast of dedication and was called by John (who wrote his Gospel in Greek) *Encaenia,* which means nearly the same as *Revival* or *Renewal.*

WHEN AND FOR WHAT PURPOSE IT IS LAWFUL FOR MEN TO ORDAIN FEASTS IN THE CHURCH; AND THE LIBERTY AND OBLIGATION IN SUCH A MATTER

TIMOTHY: On this I'd like to know if it was lawful for those who ordained this feast, and for those who followed their example, to create such a command, seeing that the Law of God makes no mention of it and that it's forbidden to add anything to it (Deut. 4:2; 13:4).

DANIEL: You have here an example of what we already discussed, by which you can judge in what case it's lawful to ordain feasts and by what means and to what purpose. For those who were the original authors of it considered the necessity of the Church and the troubles and tempests which beset it at that time and the requirements of the times, places, and persons, following the examples of the former servants of God.

Secondly, the people of God didn't make a habit of this and didn't abuse it like the superstitious and idolaters do, but they used it like a medicine, with proper moderation. We also don't read that Jesus Christ and His evangelists and apostles ever rebuked the Jews for doing this, but they instead accommodated themselves to the church of Israel in this regard.

SIX

The Day of Rest, the Foundation of Christianity

THE REASONS WHY GOD ORDAINED THE SEVENTH DAY AS THE DAY OF REST, AND WHY HE SET FORTH THE EXAMPLE OF THE CREATION OF THE WORLD IN THIS COMMANDMENT

TIMOTHY: I agree with all that you say and am content regarding the matter of laboring during the six days. But I would truly like to understand from you the reason why God chose to ordain the seventh day of the week as His day of rest instead of any other.

DANIEL: Moses didn't give any clear reason for this other than the fact that God ordained it as His example because, after having created the heaven and the earth and all that is contained in them in six days, He rested on the seventh day and blessed and sanctified it (Gen. 2:1-3; Ex. 20:11; Deut. 5:12). Thus he declares to us that the Lord wished to give us His example in order that we might be more induced by imitating Him to do what He required of us, setting it before us all our life as a perpetual image before our eyes of the creation of the world, to remind His people by it that it's from Him that we have received our birth and all that we have, and from whom we received this earth, and what Creator, Lord, Ruler, and Governor we have. He did this in order that we might never forget and might never be guilty of the reproach which He later made through Moses, saying: "Of the Rock that begat thee thou art unmindful, and hast forgotten God that formed thee" (Deut. 32:18). This consideration, remembrance, and acknowledgement is truly necessary for all, considering the grave ignorance and ingratitude which generally exists among men.

Indeed, how many people think no more of these things than the savage beasts themselves, as if they had entered into the world for their own sakes alone and with no other purpose than to live according to their own pleasure, just as the beasts? And even those who were considered the wisest and most learned philosophers and the most cunning and excellent minds of all were guilty of this—as was that renowned fellow Aristotle and others like him who denied the creation of the world and declared that it was eternal, without beginning and without end! Wasn't this a full denial of God his Creator and didn't this place the world—which is no more than a creation of His—in His place as God? How many others also have there been who consider the world itself to be god, or at least his body, and that god was its soul? And among those who believed that it was created, some have declared the angels to be the creators, while others ascribe it to some god other than the true God or to some other divine power. How many times have we also seen (and still do see) that men don't believe in His providence, which however is so joined to the work of creation that the one can't be understood or received without the other?

HOW THE EXAMPLE OF CREATION CONTAINS THE FIRST ARTICLE AND FOUNDATION OF ALL TRUE RELIGION, AND HOW THE ORDINANCE OF THE DAY OF REST OUGHT TO SERVE AS A SACRAMENT OF THIS CREATION AND OF ALL THE BLESSINGS OF GOD WHICH MEN HAVE RECEIVED BY IT

TIMOTHY: Thus this example contains the first article and foundation of the Christian religion, without which all the others have no place at all.

DANIEL: It's very clear to see. For whoever believes that God is the Creator of all things must first believe that there is only one God and that all things were created by Him. Thus none can be God but Him alone. We can thus say with the prophet: "The gods that have not made the heavens and the earth, even they shall perish from the earth, and from under these heavens" (Jer. 10:11).

Also, whoever believes this also believes that all belongs to Him alone and says with the psalmist: "The earth is the LORD's, and the fullness thereof" (Psa. 24:1). He also concludes from all this that nothing which exists proceeds from itself but that it receives all from God, and likewise that He who is the Creator can do with His creatures whatever pleases Him, and that He can do nothing but good. Therefore, no matter what He does, man mustn't become angry with Him or be embittered by His works, providence, election, or eternal damnation and predestination, and mustn't ever complain against Him. To the contrary, man must submit himself entirely to Him as his God and his sovereign Lord and Father, to whose honor and worship he must dedicate his entire life and all that he has received from Him.

TIMOTHY: This is very sensible.

DANIEL: Seeing that it is so, there was indeed a great need for this people of God (who still dwelt under shadows and figures) to have some perpetual commemoration of this (like a sacrament, as was done with the other blessings of God) to keep them in daily remembrance in order that they might not forget God their Creator and might not fall into such errors and atheistic heresies and other similar beliefs (which are infinite) concerning both the creation of the world and the beginning of all things as well as its administration and the foreknowledge and providence of God. In these things all the greatest philosophers have greatly erred and have generally given way to their own imaginations and fantasies.

Thus this command isn't of so little importance and so

little profit as it might appear at first glance. For it teaches what all the philosophers have never been able to discover or understand by all their studies and by all their inquiries and discussions. For this is a matter which can't be understood or comprehended by human reason, as the epistle to the Hebrews testifies, saying: "Through faith we understand that the worlds were framed by the word of God, so that things which are seen were not made of things which do appear" (Heb. 11:3). Thus you see how the Day of Rest assists and increases the faith of the people of God in this way.

Thus, when the Israelites labored six days, this labor reminded them of the work God accomplished in the creation of all things and instructed them concerning Him who gave them both life and strength to do what they did, and who gave them the tools with which they labored. It likewise admonished them to recognize that their work didn't proceed from their own power, reason, or ingenuity, but from God their Creator who governed them by His providence. So also it reminded them that everything they did ought to be done for His glory. Therefore all this served them as images which always placed before their eyes the power, wisdom, and goodness of God their Creator from whom they had received all these things and by whom they were what they were and from whom they received life, motion, and feeling, and that by laboring according to this commandment they conformed themselves into His image.

In short, the Day of Rest ought to have reminded them of what the Lord so often showed them by His prophets—especially Moses—when He explained to them that they didn't acquire the land in which they dwelt or the possessions they possessed by their own wisdom and knowledge or by their judgment or power and might or by their own hands or swords. But instead they received these things by the gift and the good pleasure of their God, who loved them more than all other peoples and who chose them to sanctify and separate them from all other peoples, separating them in order to dedicate and consecrate them to Himself and for His service, just as He chose to represent this to them by this Day of Rest (Deut. 8:11-18).

For this reason the psalmist said: "We have heard with our ears, O God, our fathers have told us, what work Thou didst in their days, in the times of old. How Thou didst drive out the heathen with Thy hand, and plantedst them; how Thou didst afflict the people, and cast them out. For they got not the land in possession by their own sword, neither did their own arm save them: but Thy right hand, and Thine arm, and the light of Thy countenance, because Thou hadst a favour unto them" (Psa. 44:1-3). This is what the people of Israel were to consider on the Day of Rest and throughout all their life.

Likewise we should also consider what Paul said of the blessings God sends to us: "He left not Himself without witness, in that He did good, and gave us rain from heaven, and fruitful seasons, filling our hearts with food and gladness" (Acts 14:17). He also testifies that "He giveth to all life, and breath, and all things; and hath made of one blood all nations of men for to dwell on all the face of the earth, and hath determined the times before appointed, and the bounds of their habitation; that they should seek the Lord, if haply they might feel after Him, and find Him, though He be not far from every one of us: for in Him we live, and move, and have our being" (Acts 17:25-28).

SEVEN

Meditation: A Preparation for the Day of Rest

HOW ALL THE LABORS AND SKILLS OF MEN OUGHT TO SERVE TO INDUCE THEM TO MEDITATE ON THE WORKS OF GOD AND TO PREPARE THEMSELVES FOR THE SANCTIFICATION OF THE TRUE SPIRITUAL REST

TIMOTHY: From what I can understand, God ordained labor throughout these six days in such a way that even our meditation during these days isn't only a preparation for this rest which follows but is almost like a part of some piece of it. Therefore it seems to me that if men truly understood and comprehended the teaching which is here symbolized for us, every day and all the works in which they engage themselves would serve them for fulfilling the reason why this Day of Rest was ordained. And for the same reason they have no need to seek any other images to remind them of God their Creator and of His works besides those which are set forth daily before their eyes, seeing that the entire world is nothing more than one grand temple of God, filled to the brim with images which were sculpted by His own hand.

DANIEL: It's quite certain that if the laborers who cultivate the earth knew how to meditate on the works and marvels of God in the plants, herbs, trees, and all the fruits and things which they produce, they would be marvelously moved and wholly ravished with admiration and love for God and wouldn't be able to continue in their labors without celebrating the Rest of the Lord in their heart and mind.

We can say the same of all other professions and vocations, and particularly the employments of learned men. For, without speaking of theologians—who have a greater opportunity than anyone else to daily remind themselves of the living image of God by reading the Holy Scriptures—let us consider what fine opportunity and occasion for such meditation is offered particularly to physicians, astronomers, doctors, and philosophers in this beautiful portrait and painting of this grand book of nature which they must daily set before their eyes while engaging in their professions.

HOW THOSE WHO HAVE MORE KNOWLEDGE OF GOD'S WORKS AND THE THINGS CREATED BY HIM OFTEN ABUSE THEM MORE THAN ANY OTHER AND ARE SLOWER TO ACKNOWLEDGE GOD WHO IS THE LABORER; AND THE REASON FOR THIS INGRATITUDE AND IGNORANCE

TIMOTHY: What you say is true. But I'm astonished that those to whom God has given more means and greater occasions to do what you say not only often do less than others, but what is even worse, they transform this meditation into a use which is utterly contrary to what you speak of, often turning away from God entirely and ascribing to nature all the honor which pertains to Him as though He weren't the Creator, Father, and Conductor of nature. You see what profit Aristotle, the Epicureans, and the other philosophers made of this meditation. And Pliny, who wrote such a large book of natural history and who had such a vast knowledge of it, what opinion did he give of God and the immortality of souls! Was there ever a man who showed himself more a beast than he did when he began to speak of these things? And what of Galen, that great philosopher and chief of doctors? How much did he confuse God with nature just as the others had done, as though he had forgotten God or had never even considered Him except by accident when the admiration of nature forced him to raise his eyes higher than itself?

How I wish that God would be pleased to allow no more such philosophers today who follow these wicked and evil opinions further and further instead of studying those which are more worthy of imitation. I haven't even mentioned the theologians, among whom many are so beastly and live such an atheistic life that it can't be doubted that they never think of God at all. Nor do they even consider whether they are human or beasts and whether they are rational animals (as they're accustomed to define man) or savage beasts devoid of reason.

DANIEL: What you say offers even greater confirmation of what we already discussed. For from where does this fault proceed except ignorance of the doctrine of which this commandment of rest is the sign and symbol? For, if these people had considered this in their works and studies (as we said already), they would never have proceeded as they did, but to the contrary they would have cried out and proclaimed with David: "O Lord our Lord, how excellent is Thy name in all the earth! who hast set Thy glory above the heavens" (Psa. 8:1). And they would sing with the seraphim: "the whole earth is full of His glory" (Isa. 6:3). So also they would meditate on His works just as David meditated on them in the psalm I quoted and as he sets forth for us in contemplating the universe and all this beautiful book of nature which he sets before our eyes when he says: "The heavens declare the glory of God; and the firmament sheweth His handywork" (Psa. 19:1). The rest of what is contained in this psalm says the same concerning this matter, as well as Psalm 104 and other similar ones.

And therefore in another psalm the psalmist exhorts all creatures, both in heaven and on earth, to acknowledge and praise their Creator. He not only addresses himself to creatures endowed with reason and who possess a soul, sense, understanding, and a tongue and mouth to glorify their Creator, but also to the creatures who are without understanding and who are insensible and mute, lacking both movement or feeling. For God is so marvelous in all His works—both in the creation of the world and in His providence—that the very rocks themselves must be moved to admiration and to render Him praise (Psa. 148).

What then ought men to do, and particularly those to whom God has given more understanding and who should be the guides, instructors, and light to the others? But they don't know what to do because they haven't been instructed in the school in which this knowledge is taught. And, concerning the theologians (at whom we have much greater reason to be astonished), do you know why they so badly practice their profession? It's because many of them don't pay any great heed to the subject which ought to be their chief study: the Holy Scriptures. Or, if they labor in it, they don't labor to learn how to know and serve God, but instead they do it to serve themselves as a philosophy, or just like a tradesmen serves himself by his profession. Or else they do it to display the greatness of their mind and to acquire a name among men, or to live and provide for themselves just as men do with other professions.

TIMOTHY: I think that you've truly discovered the malady. Yet God indeed won't remain without His praise. For "if these should hold their peace," the stones will cry out and convict them of their ingratitude and wickedness, just as Jesus Christ said when He reproached the scribes and Pharisees (Luke 19:40).

EIGHT

Imitating God in His Rest

HOW MAN FOLLOWS GOD'S EXAMPLE BY CELEBRATING THE DAY OF REST ON THE SEVENTH DAY

DANIEL: Now, to return to our six days, just as God wills man to imitate Him in his labor, so also He wills him to imitate Him in his rest, and desires man to rest himself on the seventh day after he has labored six in order to have more time to meditate and to imprint upon his memory what he has studied and learned in these six days, in order that by doing so he might acknowledge God and rest entirely in Him just as He also rested the seventh day after He had in six days created the heaven and the earth and everything contained in them. And, just as the meditation during these six days ought to serve us as a preparation for the sanctification of the seventh, so also the profit which we must make of the seventh in doing what is commanded ought to serve us during all the rest of the week.

For, since the Lord instructs us in His school in this day more fully than in any other, we ought to so study and profit from it that we show by our deeds—not only during the rest of the week, but also through the rest of our life—what profit we've gained from it. And we should bear testimony of this by the true mortification of our flesh and by a holy life and lifestyle.

On this we must note the order and means which the Lord took to incite us to obey His holy will. Since He is our King, Ruler, Lord, and Father, He has the authority to command, and His commandment alone ought to be more than sufficient for us. But He does even more than this, for He sets forth His own example, showing us by it what He has done and still does daily for us, in order that it might be less burdensome for us to do what He commands us, and that we might do it with greater courage.

Our Lord Jesus Christ also employs this same means when He exhorts us to be merciful and perfect and to render good for evil, following the example of our heavenly Father: "for He maketh His sun to rise on the evil and on the good, and sendeth rain on the just and on the unjust" (Matt. 5:44-48; Luke 6:27-36).

TIMOTHY: Truly our hearts would be hard indeed if we aren't moved by such lovingkindness and goodness of God which is joined to His authority and majesty.

DANIEL: We still have one further point to note on this. It is that He doesn't require us to do the same works as He did (which no one besides Himself could do, unless there were another God like He is), but He is content if we follow His example in what He commands us, conforming ourselves to Him as closely as we can, in order to declare by this that we are indeed His true children.

TIMOTHY: And yet we do the contrary, for we forsake what He commands us to do in order that we might do what He hasn't commanded.

DANIEL: It is true. Now let's return to the commandment of rest. The fact that man was created on the sixth day (which was the eve of the Lord's rest) is very suitable to the purpose at which the commandment of God aims (Gen. 1:26, 31). For man was instructed by this that he wasn't placed in the world for any other reason than to return and cleave to Him who placed him in the world and to seek his rest in Him.

Man was also taught by this that he brought nothing into the world, but instead found all that he needed already waiting there for him, and his lodging all prepared and furnished for him by Him who had bestowed it upon him (Job 1:21). Therefore he must not distrust Him or fear any dearth by submitting himself entirely to Him.

TIMOTHY: This is indeed a good point and one worth noting.

THE MYSTERY CONTAINED IN THE NUMBER SEVEN AND THE GREAT JUBILEE AND ETERNAL REST SYMBOLIZED BY IT

DANIEL: You must also note that the number seven is a perfect number; therefore it is often used to symbolize perfection. And the fact that it's so often used in this way in Holy Scripture shows us that it wasn't ordained without some mystery. For, besides it being ordained for the Day of Rest which occurs every week, God also ordained it for the rest of the land of Israel which occurred every seven years just as the weekly rest comes every seven days. It was also ordained for the celebration of the great year of Jubilee which came every fifty years—which amount of time contains seven weeks of years—that is, seven times seven years (Lev. 25:1-16; 27:16-18; Num. 36:4). This celebration appears to have been ordained to even more explicitly represent the great eternal Rest in which all other rests are joined and consummated, which we've already begun and will continue to pursue daily until we've attained that rest when the great cornet and trumpet of God will sound by the ministry of the angels and archangels, to assemble not merely a people dwelling in the land of Canaan but all the peoples of the earth, and to eternally set at liberty all the true people and children of God (Matt. 24:31; 1 Thess. 4:16).

Now, to return to this seventh day, which is the last day of the week, it is also quite suitable to represent this perpetuity of rest which we look forward to, after which we will have nothing else to wait for, seeing that it brings with itself the consummation of all things. The symbolism of the seventh day also declares to us that this rest can't be accomplished in us until the Last Day.

TIMOTHY: In listening to you I'm reminded of what Moses said in the history of the creation of the world of all six of the preceding days: "And the evening and the morning were the first day," etc. (Gen. 1). But he doesn't speak of the seventh day like this. By this it appears that he desired to show that this day of rest was ordained to represent this great and last day of eternal rest which will have no distinction between day or night like there is at present. But this will never be accomplished in us until we have passed from this life.

DANIEL: What you say seems sensible. And, even if Moses didn't have this in mind when he wrote it, yet what you say is still true. For while we live in this world we have a physical and external rest which is common to all alike (both to true Christians as well as hypocrites), which isn't a great rest, nor does it endure for any great length of time. There is another rest which is spiritual which belongs to none but true Christians, which doesn't put a stop to physical labor. And then follows this last rest when we shall have a true and eternal rest both of soul and body, and we will then possess fully and completely what we here only enjoy in part.

NINE

Have the Jewish Sabbaths and Feasts been Abolished?

THE PASSAGES IN WHICH PAUL MENTIONS THE ABOLISHING OF FEASTS AND THE OBSERVANCE OF DAYS

TIMOTHY: Seeing that this point is finished, I would truly like to learn of you how we differ from the Jews in the observance of this commandment, and in what way we are still bound to it or released from it. For there are many passages in Paul's epistles which quite openly appear to condemn and abolish all observance of days and all types of feasts.

In the epistle to the Romans he places those who make a difference between one day and another and who consider some more holy than others in the rank of those who are feeble and weak in the faith and who are superstitious (Rom. 14:1-5).

Also he wrote to the Galatians that he feared that he had labored among them in vain. And then he gives his reason for this fear: "Ye observe days, and months, and times, and years" (Gal. 4:10-11). It can't be denied that he said this because of the Jewish feasts which they were keeping.

And in writing to the Colossians he said: "Let no man therefore judge you in meat, or in drink, or in respect of an holyday, or of the new moon, or of the sabbath days: which are a shadow of things to come; but the body is of Christ" (Col. 2:16-17).

He clearly states that all these differences and observances of days—indeed, even of the Day of Rest itself—were nothing more than figures of things which have been accomplished in Jesus Christ. He therefore calls them "shadows" and calls Jesus Christ "the body"—that is, the substance, truth, and completion of these figures, which are as different from the reality which they represent as the shadow is different from the body. The shadow indeed clearly represents the form of the body and shows that the body isn't far away, but yet it most certainly isn't the body. Therefore what can we conclude from this except that the Gospel and the New Testament abolish all feasts and all distinction of days? For Paul concludes that the observance of these things commanded to the Jews are now superstitious and that those who observe them are returning to Judaism.

Now, if it isn't lawful for Christians to observe the feasts commanded by God to His people of old, why would it be more lawful to ordain new ones? For, if we must have some, wouldn't it be much better to retain what was already ordained by God Himself (and which bore with it such great mysteries of meaning) rather than ordain new ones without His express command?

THE REASONS WHY THE FEASTS IN THE OLD CHURCH OF ISRAEL ARE ABOLISHED IN THE CHRISTIAN CHURCH, AND HOW BAPTISM IS A SACRAMENT OF THE SPIRITUAL REST REPRESENTED IN THE SABBATH ORDAINED IN THE LAW

DANIEL: There are some today who argue in this way, not only against the other feasts observed among Christians (whether they be papists or others), but also against the ordinance of Sunday itself. But, if you truly understand what we've already said of the causes and reasons why the Day of Rest was ordained by God and the Christian liberty existing in such things, it will be quite easy to respond to all of these arguments.

We must also here note that we still hold some things in common with the Israelites to whom the Day of Rest was commanded, and we likewise have differences with them in a greater or lesser degree. Moses clearly revealed by these words that the ordinance of the Day of Rest was given to the people of Israel as a sacrament of the creation of the world and of the blessings which man received from God by it, and of the meditation of the invisible and heavenly things which are set forth for us by the image of visible and earthly things.

For, if God desired His people to commemorate many of His other blessings by means of such sacraments and such observances, the work of creation also deserved its own sacrament, for it is like the foundation of all the other excellent works which God made for man, which works we would never have possessed or known if the world hadn't been created. You must also understand what we said of the symbol of our eternal Rest in God and of His rest and His works in us. Now, of all this that was represented by this sign of Rest, there is nothing which isn't still observed and which requires a much more perfect fulfillment by the Christian people than by the people of Israel.

But we have something further in which we are different from them. First, we have a much greater clarity of all the matters hidden under the symbols of the Old Testament than the Jews had. Therefore we don't have as great a need to observe the Day of Rest as a ceremony and a shadow and figure as the Jews had, seeing that we see in full clarity and light what they possessed only as something hidden under a thick cloud.[1]

Second, we also have other sacraments more fitting not only to represent to us what was represented to the Jews by their sacraments and ceremonies, but also of even greater and more excellent things.

For we have our baptism, which (as we already said) is a true picture for us not only of this spiritual Rest which we have in God by Jesus Christ, but also of our regeneration and spiritual birth in Him, which is like a new creation and a blessing of God upon us (John 3:3; Tit. 3:5-7). This new creation is to be preferred over our first creation, which would have been

---

[1] *I.e.*, Christians are still required to observe the Day of Rest, but aren't they bound to the ceremonial aspects of it. Viret here distinguishes between the true moral intent of the commandment and its ceremonial aspect of a mere outward act of physical rest.

ruined by our sin except for the grace and blessing of the second in which "we, that are dead to sin, . . . even so we also should walk in newness of life" with Jesus Christ (Rom. 6:2-4). Now this new life we enjoy by the Spirit of Jesus Christ (who is the Spirit of sanctification and by whom Jesus Christ was resurrected and by whom we are sanctified and consecrated to the true spiritual Rest) ought indeed to be a sufficient reminder for us of all the other blessings we've received from God, and particularly those of the creation of the world and this spiritual Sabbath which can't exist in us except by means of it. For we can't begin to think of our regeneration and second birth without being reminded of our first creation and birth.

HOW THE OBSERVANCE OF THE DAY OF REST IS REQUIRED TO PRESERVE THE MINISTRY OF THE CHURCH

TIMOTHY: This conclusion must end by abolishing the ceremonial aspect of the Day of Rest and the feasts.

DANIEL: It is true. Hence we must now take one step even further. Seeing that through the Gospel we have a much greater light than the Jews ever had, just as it was required for the Law and the prophets to have a suitable time to exercise their ministry (just as we said), so it's also necessary for the Gospel to have its own time for its own ministry by which these great blessings are imparted to us. For we still have this in common with the former people of God, which won't be abolished while God has a Church in this world and as long as that Church is governed by the ministry of His Word. For, though all things pertaining to religion are in much greater perfection in the Christian Church (at least regarding the revelation of the grace of God) than they were in the ancient church of Israel, yet we aren't so perfect as to be able to lay aside the ministry of the Word of God; and we aren't without a body any more than the people of Israel were. Therefore we can't see God any better than the Israelites did (Ex. 33:20; 1 John 4:12). We can't obtain the knowledge of divine things like the angels do or by any other means than by this ministry of the Word until we arrive at the time when we will see not only "through a glass, darkly; but then face to face; . . . then shall I know even as also I am known" (1 Cor. 13:12). Therefore, even if some particular part of the ceremony of this commandment has been abolished, yet the commandment still remains in its entirety in general and in its proper substance.

THE DIFFERENCE BETWEEN THE CHURCH OF ISRAEL AND THE CHRISTIAN CHURCH REGARDING THE EXTERNAL OBSERVANCE OF THE DAY OF REST, AND THE CORRECT MEANING OF THE PASSAGES OF PAUL QUOTED ABOVE

TIMOTHY: In that case we will always need this ceremony until we have arrived at the spiritual Rest symbolized by it. Therefore it seems to me that it all comes down to one point, and that there is no difference except as much as the ministry of the Law and the Gospel differ from each other.

DANIEL: This difference carries with it much more than it might at first appear to you, for the Day of Rest wasn't only observed under the ministry of the Law as an ecclesiastical arrangement ordained for the preservation of the ministry, but it was also a ceremony bearing a symbol and meaning of spiritual things. But now under the ministry of the Gospel we don't fulfill the Day of Rest because of such a ceremony. For, seeing that the symbol has passed away by its accomplishment, we are now released from the observance of and subjection to the Day of Rest in this regard.

You can clearly see this by the fact that Christians don't keep the same day of the week as the Jews keep, which shows that they don't keep the Day of Rest because of its ceremony and figure. For this would truly be to return to Judaism as if Jesus Christ hadn't yet come and as if He hadn't died for our sins (in order that we might die with Him to sin) and hadn't risen for our justification (in order that we might rise with Him in newness of life as new creatures, to live in justice and serve Him as we formerly served sin). But, if we return to the Jewish keeping of it, we declare that we are still awaiting the Messiah with them. To keep their day would declare that we didn't regard Jesus Christ as being sufficient and that the teaching and sacraments we received from Him were insufficient for us.

This is what Paul preached against and condemned in the passages you quoted. For, when those whom he rebuked (concerning the observance of days) retained the observance of the Day of Rest only as an order necessary for the Church for the preservation of its ministry, he didn't condemn them but instead approved their action, acknowledging the need the Church has for preserving such order, as he himself testifies to us by his own actions. For, when he wrote to the Corinthians regarding the collection for the poor, he himself instructed them: "Upon the first day of the week let every one of you lay by him in store" for the relief of the poor (1 Cor. 16:2). By this it appears that, for the well-ordering of the Church, he retained the observance of this day in the churches he established by his ministry while meanwhile condemning the superstition of those who observed the day for other reasons (in the manner we've discussed), for this would be the same as to renounce Jesus Christ. So, according to Paul's testimony, those who renounce Him were also those who required circumcision and the other ceremonies of the Law as necessary for salvation (Gal. 2:16, 21). For such persons aren't without superstition and beliefs in meritorious works, ascribing some holiness to their works and to certain days more than others, as we still have examples of today among the Jews of our time.

TEN

How the Day of Rest Differs from Other Days

THE SUPERSTITIONS OF PRESENT-DAY JEWS REGARDING THE EXTERNAL OBSERVANCE OF THE DAY OF REST

TIMOTHY: Since you mention the Jews of our day, I would truly like to know how they handle themselves in this affair and if they are as superstitious as their ancestors who rebuked Jesus Christ for healing the poor sick people on the Sabbath.

DANIEL: They are now more so than ever. For, when Jesus Christ walked the earth, they didn't have any qualms about rescuing a sheep if it fell into a pit on the Sabbath. If this weren't so, Jesus Christ would have had no reason to mention such a fact in order to defend Himself against their slanders and convict them by their own actions (Matt. 12:11; John 7:21-23). By this He clearly showed that their condemnation of Him proceeded from an obvious wickedness and a desire to slander His works and teaching and not out of a reverence or a devotion they had to the commandment of God (John 5:15-16). But now they expressly forbid such things in order that by this they might have some pretext to accuse Jesus Christ of slander, as if He had unjustly made this reproach to their ancestors.

For the rest, though the most moderate among their teachers confess that the Day of Rest was ordained for meditating on the works of God and studying His Law, yet those who have written of the most exquisite and most perfect observance of this day say, firstly, that when the demons sense the Sabbath approaching, they flee and retire to the darkness of the mountains until the day is passed. By this they clearly show that they attribute more holiness to this day than to others as though it were holier by nature or as if God gave it some greater quality than the others and as if His holiness were bound up in it more than in any of the other days.

THE SANCTIFICATION AND HOLINESS OF THE DAY OF REST, AND THE DIFFERENCE BETWEEN THIS DAY AND OTHERS, AND THE MANNER OF SANCTIFYING DAYS

TIMOTHY: It also seems that Moses desired to express the same thought when he said that God blessed and sanctified this day.

DANIEL: This doesn't mean that He didn't also bless and sanctify the others, for He never made anything that He didn't bless and sanctify as much as it proceeds from Him. Therefore what Moses said here—that God blessed and sanctified this day—simply means (as we already mentioned) that He separated it from the others in order to dedicate it to another work and that He gave it another mark by which it was different from the others, just as the things taken for signs in the sacraments are different from others because of what they're used for.

For example, the bread and wine which we use in the Lord's Supper are no different (concerning their nature, substance, and quality) than the bread and wine we use for general purposes. Yet we consider them sanctified when they are applied to such a use, not because of any actual change in them or because of a holiness that they now possess more than they did, but simply because of what they represent and the purpose they serve, which is of the utmost holiness. Therefore whoever takes this bread and wine without considering it as anything but bread and wine wouldn't be any more sanctified than if he had partaken of any other bread and wine, and there would be no difference in it except that it would grievously offend God because of the abuse and contempt which this man would thus display toward Him and toward the things that they represented.

On the other hand, whoever partakes of them while considering the spiritual matters represented by them as he ought to would be sanctified, not by the sanctity of the bread and wine, but by the holiness of what they represent, which never fails to sanctify those who partake of it—though it be no more than bread and wine—if they don't despise the sacraments.

It's the same with the sanctification and holiness of the Day of Rest, for with regard to its nature it's the same as the other days, but it has one thing more: it has been dedicated as a sacrament to the meaning of a thing more holy than the others, and to make known to the people of Israel how God had also separated them from other peoples and nations in order to specially sanctify them—that is, to prepare and fit them for His service and to consecrate and dedicate them entirely to Himself in order that they might be a "holy priesthood," as He instructed by Moses and as Peter instructed Christians that they must be, and that God has given them this grace by Jesus Christ, as His chosen people: "as lively stones, are built up a spiritual house, an holy priesthood, to offer up spiritual sacrifices" (1 Pet. 2:5, 9; Ex. 19:6; Rom. 12:1).

Thus, if on this day a man did something contrary to what is symbolized by it, it isn't more holy or blessed to him than one of the other days, but it is even more polluted and cursed because the work that he did is more contrary to what he ought to have done. On the other hand, if he did on another day the things instructed us by this ceremony, this day would be holy to him.

Thus it's easy to see that the holiness doesn't depend on the day and that the day doesn't make the man holy, but the holy man, being sanctified by faith and working holy works by this faith, sanctifies the day. Or, to better express it, God sanctifies him through means of this faith. For, since "faith is the gift of God," we rightly give the honor to God for what is accomplished by faith since faith is the instrument to receive the sanctification that we receive of God, to sanctify both us and all which proceeds from us and issues from this source (Rom. 12:3; 1 Cor. 12:9; Eph. 2:8).

This is why at the beginning of this fourth commandment the Lord says: "Remember the sabbath day, to keep it holy," as though it were in the power of man to sanctify the day and keep it holy. And then at the end of the commandment He says that He Himself "blessed the sabbath day, and hallowed it," for it is sanctified by both God and man in the way that we just discussed. Thus the ministers of the Church sanctify this day when they purely proclaim the teaching of the Lord in the church; when they continually expound what was commanded in the preceding commandments; when they make public prayers in the church; purely administer the sacraments ordained by the Lord; and observe the ceremonies required in divine worship.

The people also sanctify the day when they reverently attend the assemblies of the Church; attentively listen to the voice of God from the mouth of His ministers; hold the teaching and the ministry in honor and reverence; and aid and assist the ministers in it, particularly the magistrates and governors ordained by God as protectors and preservers of His Church and this holy ministry, as well as its ministers.

Likewise all together sanctify it by calling on the Lord and by celebrating His holy sacraments and making profession and proclamation of their faith and religion and declaration of the unity and agreement which they have among themselves and with the entire Christian Church.

THE ERROR OF THE JEWS IN ATTRIBUTING TO THE CEREMONY AND OBSERVANCE OF THE DAY OF REST WHAT SHOULD BE SOUGHT IN GOD, AND THE VARIOUS SUPERSTITIONS THEY OBSERVE IN IT

TIMOTHY: Thus we mustn't think that the demons fear this day more than the others simply because of the day and its ceremonial aspect.

DANIEL: It's true, for the devil fears no one but God. Therefore, if God is in man, the devil fears and flees from him because of God who dwells within him. Now it's certain that God dwells in man when man sanctifies His Name, no matter what day it might be.

The Jews don't consider this but only look to the ceremonial aspect, to which by their deep superstition they ascribe this power because of the foolish superstitions with which they are accustomed to honor this day, which is reprehensible and something worthy of great scorn. For they consider that to change their clothing and foods and to speak and eat differently than any other day is the true sanctifying of the Day of Rest, for they have a commandment to eat meat and fish and to drink wine and not to fast more than six hours.

Concerning physical labor, they generally forbid it so strictly that it isn't even lawful to put an apple in the fire to cook it or to put a drop of wine on crushed mustard to prepare it or to peel a garlic clove to eat it. Nor is it permissible to remove a flea or kill a fly, wasp, hornet, scorpion, or other similar insect if you happen to be troubled or stung by them.

I could go on eternally describing other such superstitions, such as not being allowed to climb a tree for fear of breaking off a branch, or not walking on grass for fear of pulling it up, or not playing musical instruments or singing any song whatever, not even to pacify a crying baby, and other such ridiculous things.

TIMOTHY: There are enough here, and too burdensome as it is, without adding any more. But is it possible for the Jews to still be so superstitious and foolish today?

DANIEL: I don't know whether all of them are so superstitious. But at least their rabbis and teachers—if they teach what they've written—instruct them in these things concerning the observance of the Day of Rest.

TIMOTHY: I've learned from those who read their books that not only are they great dreamers and as superstitious and foolish as the papist theologians and the greatest monks and superstitious dreamers among them, but are even worse.

THE DEBAUCHERY BY WHICH SOME WHO BOAST THEMSELVES OF THE NAME OF A CHRISTIAN SANCTIFY THE DAY OF REST AND THE FEASTS

DANIEL: You see what superstitions men fall into when they are abandoned by God.

TIMOTHY: There are many among Christians who are the same as those you've been speaking of, for the majority don't consider that they are required to do anything besides feast, except to rest from their manual labors (which could bring some profit) in order to dress themselves in fine clothes and show themselves off—particularly the women—to feast and make great banquets and to eat better foods than on other days.

But there is one difference in which I would much prefer it if the Christians would do the same as what the Jews practice. I consider it very superstitious to not dare to play a musical instrument or to sing, but I consider this superstition much better than singing in the taverns or on the streets like drunkards and leaping and dancing as rogues and harlots in a brothel, and enjoying filthy jokes and passing the day and night in all sorts of games and other such frolics, which is how Sunday and the feasts are sanctified today by those who boast of being Christians.

DANIEL: You're correct, for the thing is quite unbearable and utterly unworthy of those who bear such a name. For, if God condemned the superstition and abuse which already existed among the Jews in the observance of the feasts He ordained, how will He endure these things? He certainly has a very good reason to speak as He did by Malachi: "Behold, I will . . . spread dung upon your faces, even the dung of your solemn feasts" (Mal. 2:3). And by Isaiah: "the new moons and sabbaths, the calling of assemblies, I cannot away with; it is iniquity, even the solemn meeting. Your new moons and your appointed feasts My soul hateth: they are a trouble unto Me; I am weary to bear them" (Isa. 1:13-14). This is the sentence of judgment God passes against the Jews. Wouldn't they have been much better off to have had neither Sunday nor any other feast day rather than to have sanctified them in this way?

TIMOTHY: I truly believe that the demons won't care to flee too far away when they see feasts such as this approaching.

DANIEL: Very true; for why should they flee when the feast is laid for them and when they are better served on this day than on any other?

TIMOTHY: I fear you're correct.

ELEVEN

Families and the Day of Rest

THE OBSERVANCE OF THE DAY OF REST SERVES FOR THE LOVE OF ONE'S NEIGHBOR AND THE EDIFICATION AND INSTRUCTION OF FAMILIES

DANIEL: All the things we've discussed up to this point are well worthy of being abolished. Yet we mustn't abolish what is necessary for the proper governing of the Church and for the preservation of its ministry. For this is the first point that we still have in common with the Israelites concerning the external observance of the Day of Rest, as we already mentioned. The other is the love that we owe to those who are under our charge, which is required of us particularly for two very clear reasons.

The first is because of the instruction that we owe those whom God has placed under our charge. For, seeing that they are created in the image of God just as we are and for the same purpose as we are—that is, to glorify God and to be heirs of His Kingdom—and that the same One who is our Lord and Father and the same Jesus Christ our Savior and Redeemer is also theirs, is a very good reason for us to give them as much time and opportunity as ourselves to be instructed in the doctrine of God their Father as His true children and of Jesus Christ their Savior, in order that they might attain the purpose for which they were created by God and brought into the world. By this our Lord clearly shows that in matters of religion He places no difference between the fathers and mothers of the family and those who are under their charge. To the contrary, He compels them all equally according to the charge He gave them. For, as it is written, in Jesus Christ "there is neither Jew nor Greek, there is neither bond nor free, there is neither male nor female" (Gal. 3:28).

Second, even when this isn't done, yet it's still more than reasonable to give some rest and some time and respite to those who serve us so that they can catch their breath and restore their strength which has been weakened by long labors. This must be done lest, being pressed too far, they become exhausted under the burdens they carry, or lose heart. Therefore when the Lord repeated His ten commandments in the fifth book of Moses, He expressly stated that: "In it thou shalt not do any work, thou, nor thy son, nor thy daughter, nor thy manservant, nor thy maidservant, . . . that thy manservant and thy maidservant may rest as well as thou." He also adds, "And remember that thou wast a servant in the land of Egypt" (Deut. 5:14-15). And in Exodus, when the Lord mentioned the Day of Rest among the civil and ceremonial laws, He said: "that thine ox and thine ass may rest, and the son of thy handmaid, and the stranger, may be refreshed" (Ex. 23:12).

But, before we proceed any farther, why do you think God so explicitly named every member of the family and all those who belong to it when He gave this commandment, saying, "thou shalt not do any work, thou, nor thy son, nor thy daughter, nor thy manservant, nor thy maidservant, nor thine ox, nor thine ass, nor any of thy cattle, nor thy stranger that is within thy gates"? He left out no family member which can't be easily understood to be included in this—no, not even the beasts themselves.

TIMOTHY: When we spoke of the division of the Law into two tables, you said that in the first table God set forth the commandments which more particularly concern His own person and in the second those which concern the person of our neighbors, by which He commends the love that we must have toward one another. Yet you say that in this commandment here (which is the last of the first table) He commends the love which the father of a family owes to his family, and particularly to his menservants and maidservants, which thing ought rather to be reserved for the second table, following the division that you made of the matters contained in each of them.

DANIEL: What you say in no way contradicts what we've already discussed concerning the matter you mention. For, though the point we're discussing at present concerns love toward one's neighbor, yet we don't consider this the primary purpose contained in this commandment or the main reason and chief end why God ordained it, but only a matter derived from and subordinate to its main point, as something additional which is included besides the main point. We can say the same of what is added concerning beasts.

WHY A REST FOR BEASTS IS EXPRESSLY MENTIONED IN THE OBSERVANCE OF THE SABBATH

TIMOTHY: This matter of the beasts surprises me more than any other. I understand the reason for a rest for the others, but beasts are another matter altogether. This surprises me much more than that He so expressly mentioned the menservants and maidservants and even the children of the household itself. For how can beasts sanctify the Day of Rest? And, if they can't sanctify it, to what purpose does their rest serve, and how is God glorified by it?

DANIEL: There are at least three reasons which seem to be very clear.

First, this rest for a beast includes with it the rest of those by whom he is used to labor, for the beast can't set to work alone, but he must be led and managed by men. Therefore when it's expressly commanded to let him rest, no one can then think of putting him to work or of laboring with him in it.

Second, by teaching us to be humane and caring toward beasts, we are also instructed in the humanity and equity which we must have toward mankind. And we are instructed in the care that we ought to have, seeing that God wills us to care for the very beasts themselves. Therefore I understand this to be a similar admonition to the one He gave His people when He forbade them to take the parents of the fledglings with their little ones when a bird's nest was found (Deut. 22:6-7).

Third, the Lord also willed to provide for the well-being of His people and avoid their harm. He declares that He desires nothing but their good, in order that we might better understand the good affection that He bears His creatures and particularly mankind. For, if the beast doesn't also have his rest and is pressed to too much labor, this won't be profitable for the family either.

By this God displays the care He has for us and how, in calling us to His service, far from His commandments tending toward our harm (even concerning our body and goods), to the contrary, by employing ourselves in His spiritual service and in procuring the matters that pertain to His glory and the salvation of our souls He at the same time provides us with the good necessary for us in this life also. For it often happens that in seeking gain we instead lose because of the insatiable covetousness and desire for gain that exists in the heart of man. For, if we desire to get all we can out of a man (or even a beast), and push them to their extremity, they may give their all for a moment, but then we'll receive nothing further from them because they won't be able to give any more effort than they've already given, and will be utterly exhausted. And therefore whoever desires to be well served either by men, beasts, or any other thing must spare them and treat them in such a way that they will derive a lasting profit from them. For, as long as the hen lives, you can expect eggs, but after it dies you can look for them no longer. It's exactly the same with other animals and creatures.

TWELVE

Magistrates, Foreigners, and the Fourth Commandment

THE LAW GIVEN IN THIS COMMANDMENT CONCERNING STRANGERS AND FOREIGNERS, AND THE PEOPLE OF GOD AMONG WHOM THEY DWELL

TIMOTHY: Why does He also expressly mention the strangers and foreigners who dwell among His people?

DANIEL: It is to make known:

First, that He desires His people not only to receive them but also to treat them humanely and not show any cruelty to them as the Egyptians did to the Israelites. Therefore He reminds them of their sojourn in Egypt.

Second, He also teaches the strangers to conform themselves to the laws and statutes of His people among whom they dwell, in order that they might not cause any hindrance or offense which can't be endured in the Church of God. Therefore, if the strangers are of the same religion, they mustn't be different from those of the place in the ordering of their church if the church has such an ordering which pertains to it. If however the inhabitants are of another religion and don't agree with the Church of God in all matters, they must at least beware of harming others by evil examples, and must endeavor to win them to the Lord by all possible means.

For, just as we're bound to those of our own family who are under our charge and subjection, so also we must have regard for the strangers who dwell among us, inasmuch as they must submit themselves to those among whom they dwell. For, just as the fathers of families have authority over all those who are within their house (and for this reason they must also provide for them), so also rulers and magistrates have power and authority over those who dwell in the lands and countries over which they rule and administer justice. For, even though a stranger might only be passing through the land, even so he shouldn't be permitted to do anything forbidden by God and contrary to the just and righteous laws of the country.

TIMOTHY: But, since the Sabbath was ordained for the people of Israel as a sacrament of the things you just explained, why would God desire strangers to also be bound by it even when they are of another religion? For I don't doubt that the word *stranger* in this commandment must be understood more of religious strangers than any other, seeing that in Holy Scripture those who are truly taken for strangers are those who aren't members or citizens of the holy city of God or servants of His house, which is the Church. And yet the sacraments and other similar ordinances aren't ordained for anyone except those who are the people of God.

DANIEL: Even though strangers who aren't a part of the people of God couldn't properly sanctify the Day of Rest as this people did, yet they could truly cease from labor and from conducting their business in order that they might not cause an offense to the people to whom the sanctification of the Day of Rest was commanded. For:

First, strangers couldn't conduct their labors and engage in business without the inhabitants of the country itself often being engaged in a part of the business and engaging in trade with them. Therefore, if labor and business transactions were permitted to strangers, it wouldn't have been easy to keep the residents of the country from doing business with them, which we have an example of in Nehemiah. For he testifies that "In those days saw I in Judah some treading wine presses on the sabbath, and bringing in sheaves, and lading asses; as also wine, grapes, and figs, and all manner of burdens, which they brought into Jerusalem on the sabbath day. . . . There dwelt men of Tyre also therein, which brought fish, and all manner of ware, and sold on the sabbath unto the children of Judah, and in Jerusalem" (Neh. 13:15-16). But Nehemiah strongly forbade this and "commanded that the gates should be shut," and handled the disorder very well indeed (Neh. 13:19).

Second, besides the evil example which strangers can give to those of the country by doing things contrary to the Law of God, you must also note that if we don't stop all evil where God has given us the power to do so, we render ourselves guilty of it as well. For, if an idolater, blasphemer, adulterer, glutton, drunkard, gambler, and all others who lead scandalous lives received permission and liberty in their country to live in idolatry, blasphemy, sexual immorality, gluttony, drunkenness, gambling, and to commit other such dissolute acts, it doesn't follow that we ought to permit all this where God has given us the power and authority to stop it and the charge to preserve His Law and His worship pure and entire. For, if we permit the earth in which we dwell to be polluted and soiled—either by strangers or by those of the country itself—the land won't cease to cry out to God for vengeance until the evil by which it was polluted is removed and it is delivered from such pollution.

TIMOTHY: If it isn't lawful to allow the wicked examples, vices, and sins of strangers who dwell among us or who pass through our lands and country, we can truly understand how God will deal with us if we ourselves transgress and are a wicked example and an offense to strangers and if we by our wicked works give occasion to the enemies of God and of true religion to blaspheme God's name and to slander His pure and true doctrine and religion.

DANIEL: I leave you to consider it.

THIRTEEN

The Day of Rest: The Responsibility of Fathers and Mothers

THE WAYS WE CAN TRANSGRESS THIS COMMANDMENT CONCERNING THE LOVE WE OWE TO OUR NEIGHBOR AND THE DUTY WE HAVE OF INSTRUCTING OUR FAMILIES

TIMOTHY: Seeing that it is so, we can transgress this commandment in three ways toward those who are under our charge and authority:

The first is when we press them to labor beyond reason.

The second is when we don't give them time and opportunity to worship God and to be instructed in His Word, and when we ourselves aren't on the watch for this and don't labor for their instruction.

The third is when we don't stop the evil that we can hinder or prevent.

Thus it's not enough for fathers and mothers of families to content themselves with going to church and public assemblies and to think that they have rendered their duty to their families by doing this unless they also establish such an order in their family that each of them can likewise fulfill his duty. For, seeing that they are the heads, they must indeed care for the needs of the entire body and all its members, whose government is committed to them and for whom they will answer at the judgment of God; for the blood of the souls who perish in their families by their guilt and negligence will be required at their hands (Eze. 3:18-20).

DANIEL: There is nothing more certain than what you say. And the conclusion that you make necessarily follows from what we said previously. For, since God commanded His Law to be read and proclaimed before all—indeed, even before the least of all, the menservants and maidservants and porters and pages among all the people—we can truly understand that the Lord doesn't desire anyone, no matter how small or lowly they might be in the midst of the people, to lack instruction in His Law. And by the same means we can truly consider what pleasure He has in those who aren't diligent to instruct those under their charge and those over whom they hold power and authority and to have them instructed in this Law.

Indeed, if the fathers and mothers of the family must care for the bodies of those under their charge, they must have an even greater care for their souls, and this care must be as much greater as their souls are more valuable than their bodies. Thus each father must be like a prophet, pastor, and minister of the Gospel in his own house and family and must establish such order within it that it might be like a household and church of God, in order that these fathers might also receive from God the praise and testimony that He gave to Abraham when He said: "For I know him, that he will command his children and his household after him, and they shall keep the way of the LORD," for he taught all those within his house to fear and honor God (Gen. 18:19).

For this reason He expressly stated in the commandment of the sacrament of the Passover that when the children ask their fathers and mothers what the ordinance and the ceremonies observed in it meant, the fathers and mothers must explain and make clear the things represented by it in order that by this teaching the children might learn to fear and honor God and to obey Him (Ex. 12:26-27; 13:14). By this we are all admonished of the duty we owe in such a matter to all of our own, particularly when the sacraments of our Lord are administered in the church, and above all in the Lord's Supper.

And concerning strangers, if we are required to have such care for them as we said, what must we consider of those who today boast themselves of the reformation of the Church and yet who show great reluctance to receive among them poor strangers—indeed, even their own brethren who profess the same faith and religion as themselves and for which they are persecuted by the tyrants of the antichrist and have escaped from their hands as poor sheep fleeing from the clutches of wolves?

TIMOTHY: Far from considering them Christians, I can't even consider them worthy to be taken for men, but only for savage beasts, stripped of all humanity.

DANIEL: I wholeheartedly agree with you. Yet there are many who are so barbarous and cruel, by which they openly reveal that they themselves are strangers in the house of God, seeing that they regard as strangers those who ought to be acknowledged and received as their own brethren. But let's leave this for the present and return to what we were discussing concerning the calling of fathers of families.

HOW IT ISN'T ENOUGH FOR FAMILIES SIMPLY TO REST FOR THE TRUE OBSERVANCE OF THE DAY OF REST, BUT THEY MUST ALSO DEDICATE AND EMPLOY THEMSELVES IN THE WORSHIP OF GOD

TIMOTHY: From what you say it follows that it isn't enough for us to simply give our families rest unless we also maintain a good order in which this rest is dedicated to God in the manner we've discussed.

DANIEL: It's quite true, for God doesn't command idleness by this commandment, but rather forbids it when He requires that we rest from our ordinary labors in order to free ourselves to labor in spiritual ones. For it would be much better for us to make our entire family work rather than to allow them to idle the time away, seeing that idleness is the mother and nurturer of all wickedness, as we already discussed. Therefore we must carefully note that the Lord didn't say: "Thou shalt not do any wicked work in it," but said in general: "Thou shalt not do any work."

On this we must consider that there are two types of works. There are those which are never lawful no matter what day we might do them on, seeing that they are expressly forbidden by God and are thus wicked by nature. There are also others which aren't only lawful but are also helpful, necessary, and very good, if they are done in their proper time. Now, if the Lord desires all the family to rest from these during this Day of Rest in order that what is required of us in it be not hindered in any way, what must we consider of the works which are wicked and displeasing to Him at all times?

GOD'S CHASTISEMENT OF FATHERS AND MOTHERS WHO DON'T EMPLOY THE DAY OF REST FOR THE INSTRUCTION OF THEIR FAMILIES AND WHO DON'T DISPLAY SUCH DILIGENCE IN IT AS THEY OUGHT

TIMOTHY: Yet there are many who care very little about this. And, though they allow their families to rest on this day, yet this rest serves for nothing more than to breed idleness in them and to entice them away from every good work.

DANIEL: God will reward them for this also, and will give them fair wages for their negligence and their contempt of His Word because their families are not instructed or nourished in the fear of God as they ought to be. Therefore, instead of the honor and reverence which children ought to have for them (according to the contents of the commandment following, which is the first of the second table), they are instead disobedient and rebellious. For, just as fathers and mothers transgress against this commandment in this way, so also God punishes them by their own children who despise and dishonor them just as they despised and dishonored His commandment (1 Sam 2:27-34).

It's the same with servants, who are often unfaithful and disloyal to their masters and mistresses because of their own guilt. For, because they don't take the least account of instructing their servants to serve God, God will also see to it that their servants serve them the same way the masters serve God. For it isn't possible for the blessing of God to rest on a house in which the fear of God isn't found and in which He isn't served but rather the devil. For "except the LORD build the house, they labor in vain that build it" (Psa. 127:1). And the Lord won't build if the devil is the master of the house and the father of the family instead of God.

FOURTEEN

Physical Labor and the Lord's Day

THE MANUAL LABOR COMMANDED OF GOD, AND THE PROHIBITION AGAINST MANUAL LABOR ON THE DAY OF REST, AND THE REASON FOR IT; AND ON WHAT CONDITION IT CAN OR CANNOT BE PERMITTED

TIMOTHY: Such a household truly deserves such chastisement. But, seeing that it is a question of physical rest in order that we might attend to spiritual things, I now ask you if all manual labor is so forbidden on this day that it would never be lawful to do any. And, if there is anything which is permitted, tell me what it is.

DANIEL: You can understand by what we've already said that there are no evil physical works except those which violate the Law of God and the calling of believers, which are wicked by nature and which aren't permitted on any day of the week. But all other manual labor is commanded by God except when it prevents some other more excellent and more necessary work (particularly spiritual works), for it is written: "In the sweat of thy face shalt thou eat bread, till thou return unto the ground" (Gen. 3:19). "He that tilleth his land shall be satisfied with bread: but he that followeth vain (or idle) persons is void of understanding" (Prov. 12:11). "Thou shalt eat the labour of thine hands: happy shalt thou be, and it shall be well with thee" (Psa. 128:2). "Let him that stole steal no more: but rather let him labour, working with his hands the thing which is good, that he may have to give to him that needeth" (Eph. 4:28).

Thus the evil which exists in physical labor done on the Day of Rest (which on another day isn't only permissible but is even praiseworthy) doesn't proceed from the nature of the work but from its circumstances and because of the day on which it is forbidden, inasmuch as it impedes what God particularly requires in it. Therefore it isn't evil in itself, but only because of the occasion and circumstance.

TIMOTHY: From what I can tell by your words, it seems that you wish to say that physical labor wouldn't be more wicked on this day than on any other except for the fact that it hinders the ministry of the Word of God, the sacraments, public prayers, and other things pertaining to divine worship, as well as the charity and love that we owe our families and neighbors.

DANIEL: It's true.

TIMOTHY: If this be so, it seems to me that we could then labor in our other works (as on other days) during the rest of the hours that remain after we've heard the Word of God and accomplished the other things ordained for this day.

DANIEL: There are many things to consider in what you say.

First, seeing that all the other days of the week besides this one are given for us to work our physical labors, it seems to me that we must very lightly esteem divine worship and the ministry of the Church (which we must attend to more diligently on this day than on any other) if we are unable to find the means to employ ourselves one entire day of the week in the things that God requires of us in it. For they are of such weight and consequence that we must beware in every way possible of engaging ourselves in anything—no matter what it might be—which might distract our minds from these things, in order that we might not be sidetracked or proceed half-heartedly but that we and all our family might give ourselves to it entirely without any distraction whatever.

TIMOTHY: This is quite sensible.

THE HUMANITY GOD EMPLOYS IN HIS LAW; AND HOW HE BEARS WITH HUMAN WEAKNESS IN IT

DANIEL: Secondly, in this commandment we must truly consider the great humanity which God shows His people, and how He bears with them, and what example He gives us in Himself, to instruct us to bear with those over whom we have authority and power.

First, He clearly shows us that He doesn't demand of us the full rigor of all that He might justly require of us and which by right we owe Him. For, because we've received from Him all that we have—soul, body, and goods—shouldn't we be duty-bound to employ every moment of our life in doing what He requires and commands for the true and complete sanctification of the Day of Rest? Yet we see that He assigns and permits us six days to labor for our own needs and that out of seven He only reserves one, as if He were content to have the seventh part of our time particularly dedicated and consecrated to Him, and that all the rest was for us. For, if He required of us the full weight of all we owe Him and all that He can justly demand of us, how would we satisfy His lofty justice seeing that we can't satisfy the least of all His commandments despite the fact that He relieves us of so much that we owe Him and that He bears with our weaknesses in such a fatherly way? For He doesn't treat us like subjects and servants but like weak and tender children. And even in this commandment He declares to us that we can do nothing properly of ourselves except as much as we rest in Him in order that He might work in us, such that we don't do the good that we do, but it is He who does it in us and through us. Therefore He has commanded the sanctification of this Day of Rest to instruct us in all these things by it.

TIMOTHY: Thus in doing this God has so set aside the seventh day that not only does it serve us as much as all the others, but it is also much more profitable for us if we know how to employ it according to its proper use.

FIFTEEN

God's Love Revealed in Giving Us the Day of Rest

HOW THE FATHERLY GOODNESS WHICH GOD REVEALS IN THIS COMMANDMENT TOWARD MEN OUGHT TO INDUCE THEM TO SERVE AND HONOR HIM MORE CHEERFULLY AND TO BETTER TREAT THOSE UNDER THEIR OWN AUTHORITY

DANIEL: If we truly consider all these things, they ought to serve us as goads and spurs to incite us and make us more prompt and cheerful to serve and honor our God, seeing that He shows us such fatherly goodness. For, seeing that He has relieved and released us from so much of what He could require of us, can we do any less than focus all our efforts and employ all He has given us in serving Him with a prompt and cheerful spirit and with a heart so enflamed because of the greatest goodness and lovingkindness He displays toward us? For what ingratitude would we be guilty of if of the seven parts that we owe Him, in Him giving us six, we attempt to do the very least that we can to acquit ourselves of all the duty He requires of us on the seventh day as an act of faithfulness and tribute to Him—indeed, without any harm to ourselves but rather to our greatest profit?

Further, if God—to whom we owe all—releases us from almost all the full weight of what we owe Him (in comparison with what He requires of us), shouldn't this example of His goodness and lovingkindness serve to induce us to do the same toward those over whom we exercise power and authority—just as He does to us—and to bear with them just as He bears with us, and to treat them with all charity and gentleness just as He treats us? For what comparison is there between us and Him? Can we compare the Creator to the creature—indeed, to such a miserable creature, a serf and slave of the King, the sovereign Ruler of angels, men, and all creatures?

TIMOTHY: If we truly consider what you say, we would recognize that there is no authority, lordship, or command among men that any man exercises over others which exempts us from the charity and love that we owe those under us and which exempts us from always acknowledging that we and our subjects and servants are subjects and servants of the same Lord and Master. Therefore we must treat each other as companions and brothers who must all render an account to the same Lord and Father, and we must beware of abusing the power and authority that God has given us over others, but to the contrary must use it as our sovereign Lord and Master uses His toward us, just as you explained.

DANIEL: You speak quite well. And, because we are so blind, ungrateful, inhuman, and cruel that we neither consider nor practice these things as we ought, God often sends us scourges to teach us at our own expense to have pity and compassion on one another. For, while we remain at our ease, we don't think of those who suffer, but instead we behave as the rich man mentioned in Luke who had no compassion on the poor beggar Lazarus who was full of sores who was laid at his gate (Luke 16:19-21).

So also, if we've never suffered, the adversities of others don't prick us to the heart with such keenness as when we ourselves have also experienced what they suffer. Therefore it isn't surprising that God sometimes enrolls us in the school of suffering and often sends us His scourges to teach us by them to be compassionate and merciful toward others just as we would desire them to be toward us. And therefore Isaiah said on this subject: "Hide not thyself from thine own flesh" (Isa. 58:7).

And, in the record Moses gives of this commandment in Deuteronomy, the Lord doesn't only say: "that thy manservant and thy maidservant may rest as well as thou," but He also adds: "And remember that thou wast a servant in the land of Egypt, and that the Lord thy God brought thee out thence through a mighty hand and by a stretched out arm: therefore the Lord thy God commanded thee to keep the sabbath day" (Deut. 5:15). The Lord desired His people to remember the bondage to which they were subjected in a foreign land in order that the memory of their time in Egypt might render them more caring, compassionate, and loving toward their servants, slaves, and strangers.

THOSE WHO IN THEIR PROSPERITY FORGET BOTH THEIR PREVIOUS STATE AND THEIR PAST AFFLICTIONS AS WELL AS THOSE WHO ARE IN MISERY JUST AS THEY WERE

TIMOTHY: It's no surprise if those who have never suffered but have instead always lived in all pleasures and delights aren't as compassionate on the poor people who suffer and are laden with ills. For there are even many who, after they have come out of great poverty and misery, scarcely ever think of those who are left there or whom they daily see fall into those situations.

DANIEL: These are like Pharaoh's cupbearer who, after being restored to the court of the king and to his old office, forgot Joseph whom he had left in prison in a truly miserable state, and also forgot the request he had made of him, because of the great consolation he had received (Gen. 40:20-23).

TIMOTHY: If these people deserve great blame because they don't think of relieving those who are in need and under their authority when they themselves are at their ease, but instead take advantage of them in their own repose and authority, it seems to me that the people are still more guilty who, after having been delivered from affliction and anguish and raised from their low estate to high dignity and from poverty to riches, despise the poor and not only show themselves less compassionate toward them but also more arrogant and cruel than any others over whom they have authority.

DANIEL: We experience in such people what is written in Proverbs in these words: "For three things the earth is disquieted, and for four which it cannot bear: for a servant when he reigneth; and a fool when he is filled with meat; for an odious woman when she is married; and an handmaid that is heir to her mistress" (Prov. 30:21-23). Thus because the people of Israel had been in such hard bondage—indeed, in the worst that poor slaves could be in—God truly desired to make them recognize by the commandment of the Day of Rest how their servitude had been exchanged for rest, in order that they might always keep the day in all humility before their God and in order that it might always remind them of the compassion they ought to have toward those who are also in subjection or servitude.

Therefore He willed to set forth a memorial in this commandment which would serve not only for this people but also for us. For, if we consider first what captivity and tyranny God has delivered us from by His Son Jesus Christ, and then how many miseries He has rescued us from and continues to daily deliver us from, this consideration and memory should truly move us to entirely dedicate ourselves to the works which the Lord requires of us on the Day of Rest and to give time and rest to those who are under our charge and power in order that we all together might entirely dedicate ourselves to the true sanctification of the Day of Rest and that we might all attend to the instruction of the Lord to which we are particularly called upon this day.

SIXTEEN

Despising God by Despising the Preaching of His Word

THOSE WHO PAY NO HEED TO THE DAY OF REST AND WHO DO NOT HEAR THE WORD OF GOD OR GATHER WITH THE ASSEMBLY OF THE CHURCH

TIMOTHY: To tell the truth, there are many who pass over such things very lightly. I speak of those who dwell in the very country where the Gospel is purely preached and who indeed desire to be looked upon as good Christians. I leave aside those who often pass by many Sundays without entering the house of the Lord and the assemblies of the church and without hearing the Word of God and who do none of the works for which this day was ordained. (For these aren't worthy to be taken as Christians, but rather as men without God, without Law, and without faith, or for poor brute beasts. For there is no religion, no matter how corrupt it may be—be it among the Jews, Muslims, or papists—in which a man is permitted to refrain from attending a gathering of his religion in some particular time set aside for it, to render some testimony of his religion. I am at least assured in this regard of the papist religion, for though the ignorance is as great as it is within it, yet it would still be found strange for a man to remain even two or three Sundays without hearing mass, for the papists consider this as the most important act of all their religious service.) But these of whom I speak at present don't worry themselves about rendering such obedience to the commandment of God as they render to the commandments of men, nor to show such honor for the Word of God as they show for human traditions utterly contrary to it. Therefore I leave them aside as dogs who excommunicate themselves from the Church of God and who in no way sanctify the Day of Rest.

DANIEL: You've touched on a truly reprehensible matter, for which the ministers of the Church and the magistrates ought to keep a sharp watch.

THOSE WHO CONTENT THEMSELVES WITH ONE SERMON EVERY SUNDAY AND WHO DESPISE THE OTHERS

TIMOTHY: Let's leave them alone, as I said, and speak of many others who indeed show some devotion in attending the assemblies of the church and hearing the Word of God. But, as soon as they've heard a sermon, they assume that they've done enough and have sufficiently sanctified the Day of Rest and that it's now quite lawful for them to pass the remainder of the time afterward in whatever pleases them (except in any good work which might bear some profit; for, if they labor in some such work, they think they've violated the commandment). Therefore, though they dwell in places in which many sermons are preached at morning, noon, and night, both for the great as well as the small, yet it seems that their conscience objects to hearing more than one, and particularly to hearing those which occur after dinner, as if the Word of God preached in one of them isn't preached in the others and as if one time weren't as worthy as the other. Therefore I greatly commend those who endeavor to employ the entire day either in hearing the Word of God or in doing other things necessary in it.

THOSE WHO WOULD NEVER LISTEN TO A SERMON IF SUNDAY DIDN'T COME AROUND AND IF IT WEREN'T A FEAST DAY; AND WHO DON'T EVEN HAVE THE PATIENCE TO HEAR A SERMON IN ITS ENTIRETY

DANIEL: You speak truly. But there are some who do even

worse than what you've said, for there are many of those indeed of whom we speak at present who would never attend a sermon if Sunday didn't come around and if there weren't any holy days. And yet they still don't have the patience even on this day to listen to a sermon all the way through. There are some who don't arrive until the preaching is half finished and yet who still don't have the patience to listen until it's concluded. If they come at the beginning, they scarcely pay attention until the middle of it. But above all there is an abysmal despising of prayers, even though they are made in a language that all understand and are very much shorter than the mumblings of the papist priests, which scarcely anyone can understand, even those who understand Latin!

TIMOTHY: I often find that I must guard myself from what you say, which matter greatly displeases me, for such ingratitude is very strongly contrary to the grace which God has given in our times to those to whom He has sent His Word.

DANIEL: Doubtless so.

THOSE WHO ATTEND A SERMON SIMPLY TO SLEEP AND THOSE WHO AREN'T ATTENTIVE TO THE TEACHING SET FORTH IN IT BUT INSTEAD LET THEIR MINDS WANDER

TIMOTHY: Yet what do you say of those who, besides all that you've said, only attend a sermon—when they do attend—simply to sleep, and who spend all their time (or at least a part of it) in this occupation while they are there? Can you deny that these people do indeed rest on the Day of Rest and that they keep it very well?

DANIEL: You would be correct if sanctifying the Day of Rest were the same as sprawling out so you can sleep.

TIMOTHY: We can also add to this those who, though they are

present at the sermon in body, yet their mind and thoughts are far away.

DANIEL: This is why these people (more than any others) generally find the sermons too long. For, if they diligently considered the teaching of God which is set forth in the sermon and if they were attentive as they ought to be, they would always find the sermons too short. Now there is a difference between these and the sleepers in that these are often lost in thought and have discussions in their own minds by which God is not honored at all, and which are much worse than the snores of the sleepers.

TIMOTHY: It's true. Therefore in order to sanctify this day it's truly necessary for us to be mindful of all the means by which we can employ ourselves in truly and properly serving God with both soul and body.

SPIRITUAL WORKS TO WHICH MEN CAN APPLY THEMSELVES ON THE DAY OF REST WITHOUT APPLYING THEMSELVES TO MANUAL LABORS; AND THE CONTEMPT FOR GOD'S INSTRUCTION WHICH EXISTS IN MANY

DANIEL: You can truly see that, if men desire to find a labor to employ themselves in concerning the works for which this day is particularly set aside, they will find enough without turning to those which are permitted on other days. For, even if we dwell in a place where there is only one sermon preached, wouldn't those who know how to read have a very good pastime and a very good work in reading the Scriptures and other books pertaining to their instruction or in singing the psalms and praises of God?

TIMOTHY: But not everyone knows how to read.

DANIEL: I'm well aware of that. But those who don't know how to read could spend the time in listening to those who do know how to read, if they have the opportunity to do so. And then, being together (both those who know how to read and those who don't), they could employ themselves in teaching their families and neighbors who are more ignorant than themselves. Or they could employ the time in being taught by the wiser among them. And, while the wise employ themselves in teaching and the ignorant in being taught, they could converse together on the Word of God and could employ a part of the time in prayers and visiting and comforting the sick and in other works of mercy. In this way all would find so many works to do that the day would truly be quite short. Instead of the day being tedious, they wouldn't even realize that the time had passed. Yet all these things are required for the sanctification of the Day of Rest, and are so necessary for Christians that they are unworthy to be considered Christians without them. For, seeing that we have the anointing of the Holy Spirit, because of which we are called Christians (which comes from the name *Christ* or *Anointed One*), we are required to properly fulfill the meaning of our name and to all become like preachers and ministers of the Word of God toward each other in our everyday conversations, and particularly among our households and families.

TIMOTHY: All that you say is true. But how will so many poor ignorant people do this who are not only found in villages but also in large cities, who have scarcely more instruction in the Christian religion than poor brute beasts? How will these people teach their own families when they don't know it themselves?

DANIEL: You can truly understand the answer which must be given to this by what we've already said. For those who aren't able to teach can be taught, provided that they wish to be obedient and desire to be instructed. But it's a true evil when such persons know nothing and yet still don't desire to learn, but instead despise and detest the knowledge of God.

SEVENTEEN

Labor and Idleness on Sundays and Holy Days

WHETHER IT IS BETTER TO LABOR ON FEAST DAYS AND HOLIDAYS INSTEAD OF REMAINING IDLE AND LAZY

TIMOTHY: This is the greatest evil that could exist. But, to return to the point of what physical labor can be done on the Day of Rest, do you wish to conclude that it would be better to allow those who don't occupy themselves with the spiritual works you mentioned to labor at their other works necessary for daily life rather than to remain idle or to pass the time in some vain thing or some evil work?

DANIEL: If I had the authority which the magistrates possess, I would provide for it so, if I couldn't deal with the men in a better way. For they must either labor in God's service, in some other work which wouldn't be harmful, or in one that is utterly useless. Wouldn't it be much better if those who spend their livelihood on entertainments, gambling, taverns, night clubs, and often in brothels, instead labored according to the commandments that we've already heard rather than placing themselves in poverty with their wives and children and then stealing from others, as often happens to such people?

TIMOTHY: It would be much better, without comparison.

DANIEL: Yet I always find it best to advise that the entirety of this day should be employed as much as possible in divine service and in works of mercy. For, if we were allowed to labor indiscriminately in all works, there would be a danger that little by little this day would begin to be considered just like the other workdays and that the things for which it was ordained would in time come to be despised because of the greed and wickedness of men. Therefore it's necessary for those who have more understanding of Christian liberty in this regard to bear with the ignorance of the most uninstructed.

Also, we must consider that there are some works which can always be done no matter what day it is, and others which can easily be permitted according to the need which might arise and according to the purpose for which they are done. We have an example of both of these cases in the works which were done by Jesus Christ on the Day of Rest as well as in the responses He gave to the Jews concerning them.

EXAMPLES BY WHICH JESUS CHRIST TAUGHT THAT SOME WORKS ARE PERMISSIBLE ON THE DAY OF REST

TIMOTHY: I would truly like to hear the conclusion of these examples.

DANIEL: When the disciples of our Lord Jesus Christ were rebuked by the Jews as violators of the Day of Rest because they picked wheat and rubbed it in their hands to eat it, and when Christ was also accused of the same crime because He healed the sick on this day, He set forth many very clear reasons in His own defense and in defense of His disciples (Matt. 12:1-8).

He first set forth the example of David, who in a time of need ate the showbread and gave it to those who were with him to eat as well, even though it was forbidden by the Law for anyone to eat it except the priests (Luke 6:1-5; 1 Sam. 21:2-6).

Then He gave the example of the priests who on the Day of Rest don't cease to prepare and labor upon those things necessary for the sacrifices (Matt. 12:5).

By this He declares that, when some urgent necessity arises, God doesn't desire a man to perish because of the keeping of the Day of Rest, seeing that (as Jesus Christ Himself testified), man wasn't made for the Sabbath or to serve the Sabbath, but rather the Day of Rest was made for man and to serve man. He also declared that the greater brings an end to the lesser and that the ceremonies of God must be judged according to the purpose and end for which they were commanded [Matt. 12:6].

TIMOTHY: Then you wish to conclude by these examples that it's lawful for all men to labor on the Day of Rest if there is some work to be done which can't be omitted without placing a person in danger or at risk or without neglecting the things He has commanded us.

DANIEL: Our Lord Jesus Christ goes even further than this when He answered the Jews who accused Him because He healed a man with a withered hand on the Day of Rest. He told them that they themselves worked for the benefit of their animals. For even on this day they saw no harm in rescuing a sheep or a donkey that had fallen into a pit. By this He clearly declares what He Himself said on this point—that is, that it's lawful to do good on the Day of Rest and that He desires "mercy, and not sacrifice" (Hos. 6:6; Matt. 12:7). Therefore works of mercy and charity by which we can meet the needs of our neighbors, both in their body and goods, aren't only permissible for us on the Day of Rest but are so required of us that if we don't do them we violate the Day by our superstitious observance of it and by failing in our duty against the command of God instead of sanctifying it.

TIMOTHY: This is very sensible.

IMPERIAL LAWS AND ORDINANCES ON THIS SAME SUBJECT

DANIEL: The ancient Christian emperors truly understood this liberty and issued very strong Christian laws. They generally forbade the Sabbath to be "profaned by any annoyances resulting from collections" of taxes, and commanded that all judges and magistrates and all peoples and all laborers rest on this day, saying: "No notice shall be served upon anyone; no security shall be exacted; bailiffs shall remain quiet; advocates shall cease to conduct cases, and this day shall be free from the administration of justice." Also, no one was "to devote themselves to obscene pleasures; and no one shall then demand theatrical exhibitions, the contests of the circus," and other similar pastimes customary among the pagans. It was further proclaimed that "If anyone should think that upon this holiday he can venture to interest himself in exhibitions," or if any judge or official engaged in any "public or private business, . . . he shall suffer the loss of his employment and the confiscation of his property."[1] We must understand this to refer to the ordinary work of a magistrate which could be postponed to other days without damaging the public peace.

Now, though the Christian emperors bore such reverence for this day, yet the emperor Constantine gave a law by which he allowed peasants and farmers to labor on their lands in the case of necessity, "as it frequently happens that the sowing of grain or the planting of vines cannot be deferred to a more suitable day, and by making concessions to Heaven the advantage of the time may be lost."[2] These are almost his exact words faithfully translated. Thus if the Christian emperors allowed this even on Sunday itself, we mustn't doubt that they would have permitted it much more on the other feast days which don't bear nearly as much weight as this one.

TIMOTHY: From what I can judge by what you've said, the Word of God allows all physical labor as much as it's necessary for human life and the preservation of men and their goods and which can't be delayed without great harm to them and without leaving or creating some great risk or danger, as long as it's done

[1] *Corpus Juris Civilis,* III:12:10, Samuel Parsons Scott translation.

[2] *Corpus Juris Civilis,* III:12:3.

out of necessity and not out of a contempt for the commandment of God.

WHICH NEEDS GIVE A MAN SPECIAL PERMISSION TO LABOR ON THE DAY OF REST AND THE SIN OF THOSE WHO LEAVE MANY OF THEIR WORKS FOR THIS DAY IN ORDER TO GAIN TIME ON THE OTHER DAYS AND WHO CERTAINLY DO NOT SANCTIFY THE DAY OF REST

DANIEL: But we must also diligently beware of disguising our miserliness, greediness, and our contempt for the Word and worship of God under this veil of necessity by placing under its shadow everything that pleases us. This is why Nehemiah (as we already discussed previously) so violently rebuked and utterly forbade the selling of goods which the Jews engaged in with their neighbors on the Day of Rest because of their greed (Neh. 13:15-21). Thus, if we labor for the sick and poor on this day and not to satisfy our own greed, our labor will be praiseworthy. Likewise it's lawful if the work that we do serves for the edification of the church and the advancement of God's worship, as appears by the two other examples Jesus gave the Jews on this point, the one taken from circumcision and the other from the priests. For the Jews didn't cease to circumcise on the Sabbath. Nor did their priests cease from preparing the things necessary for their sacrifices.

TIMOTHY: Following what you say, it seems to me that it would be good to take heed of many things which we must expressly beware of on Sunday, lest they greatly hinder divine worship. For it often happens that, by performing some comedy or tragedy, or by the sport of archery, crossbow, or some other pastime, the preaching of the Word of God and the greater part of divine worship is abandoned by many, and the vast majority of people give themselves to debauchery in the very places where the Gospel is preached, which is scarcely permitted even in the papacy.

DANIEL: What you say is true. But if you point this out to them they would respond that they are merely passing the time because they cannot do these things on other days lest they lose their labor. By this they reveal how much they esteem the worship of God, seeing that they prefer to leave God's work undone in order that they can do their own.

TIMOTHY: You speak truly. But certainly the command of God is not observed as it ought to be.

EIGHTEEN

The Christian Sabbath

WHY WE DO NOT KEEP OUR DAY OF REST ON THE SAME DAY THAT THE JEWS KEEP THEIRS

TIMOTHY: Now, since I'm content with all the points we've dealt with until now, there only remain two little points on which I still desire your opinion:

Seeing that the Day of Rest is still necessary for us because of the reasons you already set forth, why don't we keep it on the same day that the Jews do? Is this done simply as a rebuke to the Jews to show that we don't keep their law?

Secondly, seeing that the eternal rest we await in the perfection of the Last Day isn't yet consummated in us, why don't we also engage in the ceremonial aspects and symbols like the Jews do until it's fully consummated in us, seeing that this ceremony is like a sacrament of the creation of the world and of the blessings within it?

DANIEL: The early Christians didn't change the day simply out of a consideration for the difference between Jews and Christians. For simply to have changed the day and to have retained the superstition which the Jews keep concerning it wouldn't have been of much help. But they did it out of a consideration for the resurrection of our Lord Jesus Christ, who is the true consummation of the spiritual rest we await and the foundation of our resurrection and regeneration, which is like a new creation for us. Therefore, though this resurrection and regeneration aren't yet consummated in us, yet because they are fully accomplished in our Head, it's sensible and reasonable for the sign to cease since we have the reality, and that we content ourselves with the other sacraments which symbolize the accomplishment of all these things and which bear witness to us of much more excellent things.

TIMOTHY: I'm content with your response. Thus I gather from all that we've discussed concerning this commandment that, though the Jewish observance of its ceremony is abolished in the manner we've stated, yet we are bound to refrain from working at ordinary labors if necessity doesn't compel us in the way that we already stated, such as is required for the preservation of the ministry of the church and its well-ordering and divine worship and for fulfilling the duty of love toward those who are under our authority.

ALL THOSE WHO BY ANY MEANS HINDER THE COURSE OF THE MINISTRY OF THE CHURCH OF JESUS CHRIST GREATLY TRANSGRESS THIS COMMANDMENT

DANIEL: This is the conclusion on which we must rest, distinguishing between the ceremonial aspect of this commandment and what it retains from the law of nature printed on the hearts of all. For, laying the ceremony aside, yet our conscience indeed bears us witness that if we take for certain that there is one God to whom we owe "honor and glory," it is then necessary for us to hear His teaching and for us and ours to be mindful of this ministry which He has ordained (1 Tim. 1:17). Therefore all the passages of Scripture which mention the ministry and its ministers pertain to this commandment.

Thus it follows that not only all those who hinder but also all those who don't in every way employ themselves in advancing and aiding the course of this ministry transgress against this commandment, whether they do it in words or deeds. So also they sin who are the reason that it and its ministers are despised and that the things necessary for its preservation aren't ordered and set forth as they ought, particularly those who withhold and plunder the goods ordained for the Church for this purpose or who distribute them to false prophets, not providing for the needs of the true pastors who have the charge of teaching both the small as well as the great and instructing them in doctrine.

TIMOTHY: There are a great number of these; and I don't doubt that all are in some way included here. For there is no man, no matter how just he might be, who doesn't fail in many regards in all these things, particularly the bishops, prelates, and pastors and ministers of the Church and the kings, rulers, and officers who don't fulfill their duty in maintaining this holy ministry and the study of doctrine joined to it. And if these are guilty, how much more are those who not only cease from fulfilling their calling and duty in this regard but, which is worse, who seek to completely abolish the holy teaching and the true ministry of the Church and persecute and put to death its true ministers in order to maintain the antichrist, his false prophets, and their false doctrine, superstitions, and idolatries?

DANIEL: This is easy to judge.

TIMOTHY: There is still one point on which I would like to have your advice. It concerns the source of the other feasts (besides Sunday) which were introduced in various ways into Christianity. But I fear that we'll have to return to this point at another time because it would take too much time and I would weary and detain you too long at present. Therefore I'm content to let it alone for the moment.

DANIEL: You wouldn't weary me, but on my part I am also content to go no further at present because I can show you a conversation which some of our friends had concerning this point among other things, by which you can understand all that you desire to know.

TIMOTHY: That's good enough for me, along with what you've already sufficiently said in the present conversation.

NINETEEN

The True Meaning of the Sabbath

A SERMON BY JOHN CALVIN

"Keep the sabbath day to sanctify it, as the Lord thy God hath commanded thee. Six days thou shalt labour, and do all thy work: but the seventh day is the sabbath of the Lord thy God: in it thou shalt not do any work, . . ."
— Deuteronomy 5:12-14

After speaking of worshipping and serving God purely and of glorifying His name without using it in any vain oaths or any other things except in honor, He now mentions the worship of God according to what He has required in His Law, and of the order that He instituted in order that believers might exercise this worship.

First, the Sabbath or Day of Rest was in part a figure to show that men can't serve God rightly without mortifying all that exists of their own nature and without dedicating themselves to Him in such a way that they might be as it were entirely separated from the world.

Secondly, the Day of Rest was a ceremony to bring the people together in order that they might hear the Law, call on the name of God, and offer sacrifices and all other things pertaining to spiritual worship and order.

Thus we see how the Sabbath Day was spoken of; yet we won't properly understand it without making this distinction and without dealing with these two parts separately and in detail.

Therefore we must note that the Sabbath or Day of Rest was a shadow under the Law until the coming of our Lord Jesus Christ to symbolize that God requires men to utterly rest from their own works. And this is what I meant in one word when I said that we must mortify all that exists of our own nature if we desire to be conformed to our God.

Now, as proof that this is so, Paul declares it; and besides this we have records of it in the New Testament. But it will suffice to quote the most obvious, which is in Colossians, where Paul says that we have the substance and the body of those things foreshadowed under the Law. We have it, he says, in Jesus Christ (Col. 2:17). And therefore the Day of Rest as well as various other ceremonies were used to train the fathers of old in this hope. But, now that the reality itself is given to us, we mustn't rest in shadows any longer. It's true that the law isn't abolished in such a way that we ought to reject the substance and truth of it, but yet the shadow is abolished by the coming of our Lord Jesus Christ (Matt. 5:18; Eph. 2:15; Col. 2:14-17).

Someone might ask how the fathers of old knew this. Moses explained it to them, as we see clearly in the book of Exodus. For, after God published His Law in the twentieth chapter of Exodus when He revealed it to Moses, He then told him to what purpose it tended, and said that He had ordained the Sabbath Day as a sign that the people of Israel were to be sanctified unto Himself (Ex. 13:13-17). "It is," He says, "the mark of My holiness which I have instituted among you."

Now, when the Scripture speaks to us of being sanctified to God, this means to separate ourselves from all things that are contrary to His service. But where is such purity to be found? We are in the world and we know that in this world there is nothing but wholesale perversity and wickedness, just as John mentions in his epistle (1 John 5:19). There's no need for men to go outside of themselves to battle against God and His righteousness, for all our mind and all our desires are at enmity against God, as Paul says (Rom. 8:7). When men give free rein to their own thoughts, desires, inclinations, and lusts, they make open war against God.

We know how Genesis states that every imagination of man is utterly wicked and that all that man ever devises within himself and whatever he brings forth from his own store is utterly perverse and corrupt before God (Gen. 6:5).

So then we clearly see that we can't be sanctified to our God—that is, we can't serve Him in purity—unless we are separated from the defilements which are contrary to Him, which means that whatever is of our own nature must be destroyed. Now it was necessary for all these things to be symbolized to the fathers of old because Jesus Christ wasn't yet fully revealed to them. But today we have in Jesus Christ the full accomplishment and performance of all these things. And, as proof of this, Paul says that the old man is crucified with Him (Rom. 6:6).

When Paul speaks of the old man in this way he means the things that we inherited from Adam, all of which must be abolished and done away with. This isn't referring to the substance of our body or soul but only to the wickedness within us. This is the blindness that makes us go astray and the wicked lusts and desires which are utterly contrary to God's righteousness. All of this, because it's drawn from Adam, must be cast down.

And how is this done? It isn't by our own power or might but by our Lord Jesus Christ who, by dying for us to wash away our sins so that they might not be imputed to us any longer, has also purchased us this privilege, that by the power of His Holy Spirit we are able to forsake the world and ourselves in such a way that our fleshly desires won't rule over us (Rom. 6:4-5; 1 Cor. 15:3). And, though we are full of disobedience and rebellion, yet God's Spirit will overrule us and hold down our lusts and keep them in subjection. And therefore it's said that we are risen again with Him, just as Paul declares (Col. 2:12).

But this wasn't yet revealed under the Law. Therefore it was necessary for the fathers who lived at that time to have some help (such as the sacrifices were) to support them in the hope of the death of our Lord Jesus Christ in order that they might know that their sins were cleansed by the blood of the mediator. Likewise they had the Day of Rest as a testimony of the grace that was purchased for us to mortify all our thoughts and desires in order that God might live in us by the power of His Holy Spirit (Gal. 2:19-20).

Now we've laid somewhat of a foundation so that we can understand what was briefly mentioned previously—that is, that the Day of Rest was like a figure to represent what was accomplished in deed at the coming of our Lord Jesus Christ. And therefore let's carefully note that the Day of Rest extended to the whole worship of God, to show that men couldn't honor Him purely except by renouncing themselves and by being separated from the defilements of the world and of their own flesh.

This is the reason why the prophet Ezekiel also rebuked the Jews for not keeping the Day of Rest (Eze. 20:21; 22:8; 23:38). Now he says this as if they were guilty of breaking the entire Law in general. He didn't do this without good reason, for whoever despises the Day of Rest has (as much as he is able) trodden underfoot the entire worship of God. And if the Day of Rest isn't observed, all the rest of the Law is worth nothing, according to what Isaiah the prophet says. He declares that men must forsake their own pleasures and be content to forgo them or else they don't keep the Lord's rest; neither will He approve of or accept them (Isa. 58:13).

By this we see that there's no use in simply observing the ceremonial aspect alone. For, even if the Jews had most strictly kept the ceremony by assembling together on the Day of Rest without stirring a finger in their household business and yet in the meantime they cultivated their own wicked desires and pleasures and afterward put them into effect, this would have been nothing more than a mocking of God by abusing His name and by defacing and falsifying the entire order that He had instituted, which is exactly what He reproaches them for doing. But the main point was to have an eye to the true meaning of the sign or symbol—that is, to the spiritual worship of God. And yet at the same time it was also necessary for the Jews to keep the ceremony which was commanded them. For God placed a hedge about them in such a way that He didn't choose to give them the substance of the things alone, but instead willed that they also have the shadows with them until the coming of our Lord Jesus Christ.

Now by this we see what Paul mentions, which is that we are no longer tied to the old bondage of observing the Sabbath (Col. 2:20). For we must render Jesus Christ the honor of contenting ourselves with what He has accomplished for us in His own person without resting any longer in the outward things under the Law. Now we see how the observance of this concerns us today. Concerning the ceremonial aspect, it is past (as I said), and therefore we must proceed to the substance, which is that, in order to serve God well, we must learn to deny all our own will and all our own thoughts and desires. And why? Because when we think that we're wise by imagining or dreaming up this or that way to serve God, we ruin everything. Therefore our own wisdom must be thrown away and we must listen to God speak, without following our own will or imagination.

Thus the first way to keep the Day of Rest as we ought to isn't to believe whatever seems good to us, for we must rest. And how must we rest? We must remain still in such a way that our thoughts don't go running abroad to invent one thing or another. We must, I say, continue quietly in the obedience of our God. And when we are tempted by our own wishes, we must realize that these are just as much enmity against God as all our wicked and rebellious desires (Rom. 8:7). Therefore we must rest content in this regard and must surrender ourselves to God so that He alone might work in us and guide and govern us by His Holy Spirit.

By this we see that God overlooked nothing when He ordained the Day of Rest. And, since it has so vast an application, what more could we wish for to teach us a perfect doctrine of holiness than the things which the Holy Spirit has set before us? It's simply a matter of walking holily in the obedience of our God. And how is this to be done? Only by receiving His Word alone and by seeking to conform ourselves to His righteousness. Now, because the things we possess in our own nature are contrary to this, we must begin by renouncing or denying ourselves (Matt. 16:24; Luke 9:23). When this is done, won't we have everything necessary for the worship of God? But this is very difficult to do. And therefore when we hear that God commands us to keep the Day of Rest, let us pay diligent heed to it and consider that it won't be accomplished by half-hearted endeavors or by play-acting, but we must force ourselves to it. We will have profited greatly all our life if we keep it properly, by renouncing everything of our own and by dedicating ourselves entirely to our God.

And we ought to be even more inflamed to the spiritual observance of the Lord's Sabbath, seeing that we are set free from the slavish subjection of the law and seeing that God has granted us a greater privilege than He did the fathers of old, for He is content with our mortification of the old man in order that we might be renewed again by the power of His Holy Spirit, and we are no longer bound to the ceremony that was so strictly kept under the law. Considering the fact that God handles us so lovingly, this ought to bind us even more to the keeping of the principle in order that we might observe it properly.

Yes, and we mustn't excuse ourselves by saying that the Israelites had the ceremony to inspire and quicken them, which served them as a goad. For, because our Lord Jesus Christ has appeared to us, we have much more than the outward and visible sign, for in Him everything that was figured in those shadows is accomplished (Col. 2:17). Thus we mustn't desire any longer the things that were under the law. Thus you see how the thing that is ordained here concerning the Day of Rest is now fulfilled, at least concerning the truth of the figure which the fathers only possessed in shadow.

And, concerning the deed, what was commanded concerning the Day of Rest most certainly belongs to us as well as to them. For we take God's Law in itself and we have an everlasting rule of righteousness in it (Psa. 19:7-9; Matt. 5:18). And it's certain that under the Ten Commandments God intended to give a rule that would endure forever. Therefore we mustn't think that what Moses says of the Day of Rest is needless for us—not that the sign or symbol still remains in force, but we have the reality of it. And this is also why the apostle in the epistle to the Hebrews applies the things that were spoken of the Day of Rest to the instruction of Christians and of the new Church (Heb. 4:3-10). For he shows us that we must conform ourselves to our God, and that in this our utmost happiness and perfection is found because the whole sovereign good of man consists in being created in the image of God.

But, seeing that this image is defaced by sin, what can we do now to repair it again? You see then that the way for us to attain to perfection is to conform ourselves to our God and His will and to study His works so that we might do the same. Therefore we must understand that, in order to serve God well today, we are commanded to employ the utmost of our power to subdue our own thoughts, will, and desires in order that God might reign in us and rule us by His Holy Spirit. And therefore it's useless for every hypocrite to gloss over or attempt to put a fair appearance on his deeds. For, as long as wicked covetousness lies lurking in their hearts, as long as they are full of envy, bitterness, selfish ambition, cruelty, or deceit, it's certain that they do nothing but transgress and violate the Day of Rest. Therefore we must conclude that they overturn and overthrow the entire worship of God, just as I previously quoted from Ezekiel. The same is also spoken in Jeremiah (Jer. 17:24).

And indeed this is the reason why the ceremony was so strictly enforced under the Law. Do we truly think that God ever took pleasure in men's idleness? No, certainly not. But He punished the man who labored on the Sabbath Day with the same severity as if he had murdered a man (Num. 15:32-35). And why did He do this? It seems very cruel to put a man to death simply for cutting a little wood on the Sabbath Day, as though he had committed murder. Yet, despite this, God condemned him to death for cutting wood on the Sabbath Day. Why? It was because He, under this sign and figure, included the entire worship of God.

This is also why it's said in Jeremiah: "Take heed to

yourselves, and bear no burden on the sabbath day, nor bring it in by the gates of Jerusalem; neither carry forth a burden out of your houses on the sabbath day, neither do ye any work" (Jer. 17:21-22, 27). Why? It might seem that God puts too much weight on a trivial and insignificant matter; but He had a regard for what was symbolized and prefigured by the Sabbath Day. When that was despised by the Jews in this way, this was a sacrilege and treachery by which they showed that none of the Law meant anything to them.

Thus, to return to ourselves, seeing that we aren't so strictly bound to this figure nowadays and that God has given us a greater liberty which was purchased for us by the death and passion of our Lord Jesus Christ (Col. 2:14), let us learn to give ourselves earnestly to Him and to understand (as I said before) that, no matter how much we might labor in all the rest of the Law, yet it will all count for nothing unless our desires and will are so bridled that we strive to renounce all our own thoughts and desires in such a way that God has our complete submission and we declare that we desire nothing other than to rest in Him.

This is also why God sets Himself forth as an example. For He isn't satisfied with simply commanding men to rest, but He also shows them how to do it. For, after He created the world and everything in it, He rested Himself (Gen. 2:2). He didn't do this because He was weary or had any need of rest, but to draw us to study and contemplate His works in order that we might rest in them and also pattern ourselves after Him.

Thus do we desire to keep this spiritual rest? Just as it's said that God rested from His works, so we must also rest quietly, ceasing to do what seems good to us and whatever our own nature desires. If this example of God doesn't provoke us to this, we clearly show by this that we neither seek nor in any way desire our own good but that we prefer to willfully remain in our poverty and wretchedness.

As I said previously, man's sovereign good is to cleave to God and to be joined to Him. Thus you see that our Lord calls us to Himself and tells us that we can have no true holiness or union with Him except by resting from our own works. If we are always impatient and fidgeting and are always occupying our arms and legs and are still doing what we think good, we most certainly break the bond that exists between God and us and we separate and estrange ourselves from Him as much as we are able. And don't you see that by doing this we are asking to be left as a prey to Satan to be carried away by him and lost because we're no longer under the protection of our God?

But why do we do this? There are very few who give this any thought. We see the liberty that everyone gives themselves in this. If someone comes and tells a man that he mustn't walk according to his own desires and imagination, he'll reply: "Oh, I know how to look after myself." But a man couldn't invent a better way to openly despise God than by such rebellion. This is just the same as if we tried to show that we wished He didn't have any authority over us. It's true that men won't admit that this is so. But it's true just the same. For (as I said already) we aren't serving God unless we begin by denying our own thoughts and desires.

Therefore when men desire to be self-wise and to trust in their own mind so that they can give themselves the license to do whatever they want and to follow their own desires and imaginations, and when they don't labor to repress their own desires but are instead offended when others try to call them to repentance, this is a sign that they never knew what it means to serve God, which is the main point of the entire Law. And therefore let's truly note that, when God gives us His own example, He does this to gently allure us to observe the spiritual Sabbath or Rest and in order that we might realize (as I said previously) how unhappy we will be when we are separated from Him. And this is the bond of this union, which is that we might not withdraw ourselves from His religion and truth but might allow ourselves to be governed by Him.

But now it might be asked why the Jews were commanded to rest only on the seventh day, for we mustn't only deny our own thoughts and desires for a single day a week but we must instead continue in this practice every day of our life. In short, the rest that God commands us is perpetual and isn't intermittent, as they say. Why then did He only choose one day of the week? This was to show us that, when we have used our utmost endeavors to renounce and deny our wicked lusts, hypocrisies, and everything else within our own nature, yet we will never be able to attain to full perfection until our flesh is entirely removed.

It's true that believers ought to keep a continual Sabbath all their lives by refraining from their own wills and works and by seeking to dedicate themselves to God with all humility and submission so that they might be willingly obedient to Him. We must do so, I tell you, or else all the service that we desire to render to God will be no more than a pretense, and He will reject and condemn it. Yet we can never so fulfill our duty by denying our desires in such a way that there won't always be something worthy of blame in us. Paul indeed boasts that thc world was crucified to him and he to the world, but yet he still never ceases to say that his flesh battles against his spirit in such a way that there is never any agreement between them (Gal. 5:17; 6:14). And he even confesses in Romans that he felt such strife continually within himself that he didn't do the good that he desired to do. That is, he didn't perform the good with such an ardent desire as he ought; nor was he so fully determined to walk according to the will of God but that he always found some obstacles to hinder him so that, instead of running strongly, it appeared to him that he only stumbled forward (Rom. 7:15-19).

Seeing that it is so, let's note that God's ordaining of the seventh day to rest in wasn't done without cause, for by this He shows us that we can't attain to that perfect holiness which He requires of us in one day or even in a month. Why is this? It's because of the fact that, even when we've battled as strenuously as we can against the desires of our flesh and against our wicked thoughts, some residue will always remain until we are fully united to our God and until He has gathered us up into His heavenly kingdom. Until that time we will always have some temptations, troubles, and agitations within ourselves, so much so that we can readily perceive (at least those of us who truly seek to serve God) that we are still subject to many temptations and that we still experience many goads by which we are enticed to one thing or another (Rom. 7:24). And aren't all these things so many hindrances to hold us back from this spiritual rest?

If a man were resting in God as he ought to be, he wouldn't conceive or imagine anything at all in his mind that might turn him aside from the right way. He wouldn't have any wicked lusts or desires. All such things would be far from him. Thus, when we conceive various wicked or unclean thoughts or fancies, by this Satan assails us and troubles us with restlessness or dissatisfaction. And, when our mind is once inclined to do evil, there are many things within us that encourage us and press us onward in that pursuit. Even though we hate the evil, yet it happens that by such temptations we are enticed to pursue it. And by this we see that it's no easy matter to pull ourselves away from our wicked lusts and to prevent them from reigning in us any longer. Thus let us press forward with this endeavor of keeping God's spiritual rest, for we will never fully attain it until our life is at an end.

Now by this we are reminded of two things. First, we ought to loathe ourselves and to mourn continually because, even though it might appear to us that we have taken great pains to obey our God, yet despite this we recognize that we've still only begun to walk and we still fall far short of fulfilling what is required and commanded in the Law. Thus we have good reason to humble ourselves because God will always find enough (and too much) to condemn us regarding our service to Him, and also because this spiritual rest in us isn't yet such as He has commanded—indeed, it doesn't even begin to come close to what He has commanded.

Secondly, just as we have good reason to humble ourselves and to repent with true repentance, so also we ought all the more to be moved and quickened to press forward since we see our own shortcomings. "It's true," we might say, "that God has given me the grace to desire to serve Him, but how do I behave myself in this regard? Alas! I'm still very far from fulfilling it."

Since we see that this is so, what can we do but constrain ourselves to do this? Therefore, while abhorring this evil within us, let's also be the more earnest to always profit from this rest and to advance in it, and let each of us daily call himself to account. You see then how God, after having given us reason to humble ourselves every day of our life, shows us that we must be ever more and more earnest in correcting our sins and in mortifying our flesh. We must realize that it isn't enough for us to crucify our old man only in part, but instead we must be fully buried with Jesus Christ, just as Paul mentioned in the passage we already quoted (Rom. 7:4). This is what concerns the seventh day which is here spoken of.

Now we must come to the second point, which is that the Day of Rest was an institution or ordinance for believers to use to engage in the worship of God (as I already said). For that day was ordained for men to assemble together to hear the teaching of the Law preached, to partake together in the sacrifices, and to call on the name of God. Concerning these points, we hold them in common with the Israelites of old. For, though the figure has ceased (I mean the same that Paul speaks of in the epistle to the Colossians) yet, despite this, all that concerns the ordinance still continues and has its use. And what is this order and ordinance? It is that we might assemble together in the name of God. It's true that this ought to be done continually. Yet, because of our infirmity (or else because of our slothfulness), it was necessary for one particular day to be chosen.

If we were as earnest in serving God as we ought to be, we wouldn't appoint one day of the week only, but we would all gather both morning and evening without a written commandment in order that we might be edified by God's Word ever more and more. And truly this exercise is more than needful for us seeing that we are so inclined to evil that we lack nothing to turn us out of the way; thus we have need of assembling together daily in the name of God. But what do we see? We see that people will scarcely even come together on Sunday, and that most of them must be held together almost by force. Thus, considering that such infirmity exists within us, we must recognize that this order wasn't only given to the Jews in order that they might have some particular day on which to gather together, but it was also given for us, so that it belongs to us as well as to them.

But yet we must note that this isn't all, for it would be a very feeble command which only ordered us to rest our hands and feet and applied to nothing more than this. What then? We must apply this rest to a much higher purpose. We must refrain from our own business which might hinder us from meditating on God's works, from calling on His name, and from exercising ourselves in His Word. If we spend Sunday in revelry and in play and games, will God be truly honored by this? Isn't it a mockery and even a profanation of His name? But when the shop windows are shut on Sunday and people don't travel as they do on other days, this is done so that we might have more leisure and liberty to attend to the things that God commands us, which is to be taught by His Word, to meet together for the confession of our faith, to call on His name, and to partake in His sacraments. This is how this order ought to serve us.

But now let's see if those who call themselves Christians behave themselves in this way as they ought to. Indeed, a large number of them think that they can use Sunday to follow their own business, and they reserve this day as if there were no other day for them to employ for this in all the rest of the week. And, even though the bell rings to call them to the sermon, yet it seems to them that they have nothing else to do besides thinking on their business and totaling up their accounts concerning this or that matter.

Others fall to gluttony and shut themselves up in their houses because they dare not show an open contempt for Him in the streets; but yet Sunday is to them nothing more than a retreat to distance themselves from the church of God. And by this we see what desire we have for true Christianity and for the worship and service of God, seeing that we take what was given to us as a help to bring us nearer to God and instead use it as a means of further distancing ourselves from Him. And what happens when we stray? Then we retreat from it entirely. Isn't this a devilish wickedness of men? Yet this is such a common thing that it's a pity to see it. How I wish that examples of this were more rare and harder to find! But we see how all holy things are despised, so much so that most people have no regard at all for the keeping of this day which was ordained to withdraw us from all earthly cares and affairs in order that we might give ourselves entirely to God.

Also, we must understand that Sunday wasn't only instituted for going to the sermon. It was also given in order that we might apply the rest of the time in praising God. This is certainly true. For, though He feeds us every day, yet we don't sufficiently meditate on the gracious blessings that He gives us; nor do we magnify them. It's true that it would be a very poor thing if we only acknowledged God's blessings on Sunday. But, because we are too preoccupied with our own affairs on the other days, therefore we aren't as prone to worship God in them as we are on the day which is entirely dedicated to this.

Thus Sunday ought to serve us as a tower in which we can mount up to view God's works from afar when we have nothing else that hinders us or occupies our minds, so that we might employ all our thoughts to consider the blessings and gracious gifts that He has bestowed on us. And, if we can properly practice this (that is, if we can consider God's works properly) on Sunday, surely we will be more prone to it all the rest of the week after, and this meditation will as it were prepare and polish us beforehand so that our early contemplation of His works will lead us to yield thanks to our God on Monday and all the week following.

But instead of this the Lord's Day is spent not only in games and pastimes full of vanity but also in things so utterly contrary to God that it appears that men think they haven't kept Sunday holy unless they've offended God in many different ways. When the holy order which God instituted to draw us to Himself is profaned in this way, is it any wonder that men behave themselves like beasts all the rest of the week? What then is to be done? We must understand that it isn't enough for us to simply attend some sermon on Sunday in order to receive some good instruction and to call on God's name, but we must also digest these things and focus all our mind and senses to better consider the gracious things that God has done for us. And by this means we reform ourselves in such a way that on Monday and all the rest of the week we have no trouble thirsting after and longing for our God, and we don't forget to bear in mind what we learned on Sunday in our time of leisure in order that our mind might be void of anything that might hinder or prevent us from recognizing and acknowledging God's works.

Thus you see what the order is that we must observe on this day. We aren't required to keep the ceremonial aspect as strictly as was required under the bondage of the law, for we no longer have the figure or shadow anymore. But it serves to call us together so that according to our infirmity we might be exercised to better apply ourselves to the worship of God and to dedicate the entire day to Him in order that we might utterly retire from the world in order that this time with Him might benefit us all the rest of the week, as we said before.

We should also note that it isn't enough for each of us to meditate on God and His works on Sunday alone by ourselves, but we must meet together on some particular day to make a public profession of our faith. Indeed, this ought to be done every day (as I said before), yet, out of consideration for men's inability and because of their laziness, it's necessary to have one special day entirely dedicated to this.

It's true that we aren't bound to the seventh day. Neither in fact do we keep the same day as was appointed to the Jews, for that was Saturday. But, in order to show the liberty enjoyed by Christians, the day was changed because Jesus Christ in His resurrection set us free from the bondage of the law and cancelled our obligation to it (Col. 2:11-14). This was the reason why the day was shifted. But yet we must still observe the same order of having some day of the week, whether it be one or two (for that is left to the free choice of Christians). Nevertheless, if a people assemble to have the sacraments administered and to offer public prayers to God, to show their agreement and unity of faith, it's convenient and fitting to have some particular day specified for that purpose. Thus it isn't enough for every man to withdraw himself into his own house—whether it be to read the Holy Scriptures or to pray to God—but it's necessary for us to gather in the company of fellow believers and there show the unity which we have with the entire body of the Church and celebrate this order which our Lord has so established.

But what do we see happen? The despising of God's worship is a matter of common knowledge. For (as I mentioned previously) aren't there a great number of people who truly reveal that they only mock God and that they would gladly be exempted from this common law? It's true that they may attend church five or six times a year. And why do they do this? Simply to mock God and all His teaching. They are most certainly swine who come to defile God's temple, and are worthier to be in a pigsty than there, and they would do much better if they kept themselves at home in their stinking hovels. To be short, it would be better if such rascals and filthy villains were entirely cut off from the church of God than that they should come and intermingle in the company of the faithful. But yet how many times will they come there? The bell may ring as much as it likes; if you look where they take their place, you'll see it.

So then we ought to be much more diligent and careful in arousing ourselves to make such profession of our faith so that with one common consent God might be honored in our midst. Also all superstitions and idolatry must be banished. For we see that in the papacy men think they can serve God by idleness. But we mustn't celebrate the Day of Rest in that way. But, in order to apply it to its right and lawful use, we must consider (as I said before) how our Lord asks nothing except that this day be spent in hearing His Word, offering public prayers, making confession of our faith, and partaking of the sacraments. These are the things that we are called to. Yet we see how all things have been corrupted and confounded by the papacy. For, just as they've allotted days for honoring their saints and have made them into idols, so also they've assumed that they ought to be worshipped with idleness.

But, seeing that the world is so given to corruption, we must be even more diligent to properly heed this declaration concerning the Day of Rest as it's here recorded by Moses. And let us consider to what end and purpose our Lord commanded the people of old to have one day in the week to rest in, in order that we (knowing in what way this was abolished by the coming of our Lord Jesus Christ) might dedicate ourselves to spiritual rest—that is, dedicate ourselves entirely to God by renouncing and forsaking all our own thoughts and desires.

Also, let us retain the outward order as much as is necessary and suitable for us—that is, of forbearing to labor at our own affairs and worldly businesses in order that we might completely free ourselves to meditate on God's works and exercise ourselves in the consideration of the blessings that He has given us. And, above all, let us strive to acknowledge the grace that He offers us daily in His Gospel, that we might be strengthened in it ever more and more. And, when we have employed Sunday in praising and magnifying God's name and in meditating on His works, let's show throughout the entire week following that we have profited from it.

Now let us kneel in the presence of our good God in acknowledgement of our sins, praying Him to make us feel them better than we have previously. And, because we can never serve Him until the perversity and wickedness within us is destroyed and because He has shown us that we will never cease to battle against His righteousness and justice as long as we allow ourselves to be led by our own lusts and imaginations, may it please our good God to grant us such grace by the power of His Holy Spirit that we might be fully conformed to Him who died and rose again for us in order to mortify us and to bring us into new life. So then let us bear the mark of our Lord Jesus Christ by renouncing ourselves, and let us so submit ourselves to His will that we ask nothing from Him except to be conformed to His righteousness and justice in order that His law might be fulfilled in us, even as it is spiritual, and that we might be changed from flesh to spirit, to live in His obedience. And, because there is always so much in us to be condemned, may it please this good God to bear with our infirmities until His rest is fully accomplished in us and until He has taken us up into His heavenly kingdom. May it please Him to grant this grace not only to us but to all peoples and nations on the earth.

www.ingramcontent.com/pod-product-compliance
Ingram Content Group UK Ltd.
Pitfield, Milton Keynes, MK11 3LW, UK
UKHW041852190726
13854UKWH00002B/848